HOW TO MAKE
REAL MONEY
IN **SECOND**
LIFE

HOW TO MAKE REAL MONEY IN SECOND LIFE®

*Boost Your Business,
Market Your Services,
and Sell Your Products
in the World's Hottest
Virtual Community*

ROBERT FREEDMAN

New York   Chicago   San Francisco
Lisbon   London   Madrid   Mexico City   Milan
New Delhi   San Juan   Seoul   Singapore
Sydney   Toronto

The **McGraw·Hill** Companies

1 2 3 4 5 6 7 8 9 0 DOC/DOC 0 9 8 7

ISBN-13: 978-0-07-150825-4
   MHID: 0-07-150825-2

Design by Mauna Eichner and Lee Fukui

This publication is designed to provide accurate and authoritative information in regard to the subject matter covered. It is sold with the understanding that neither the author nor the publisher is engaged in rendering legal, accounting, or other professional service. If legal advice or other expert assistance is required, the services of a competent professional person should be sought.

> —From a Declaration of Principles jointly adopted
> by a Committee of the American Bar
> Association and a Committee of Publishers

McGraw-Hill books are available at special quantity discounts to use as premiums and sales promotions, or for use in corporate training programs. For more information, please write to the Director of Special Sales, Professional Publishing, McGraw-Hill, Two Penn Plaza, New York, NY 10121-2298. Or contact your local bookstore.

Second Life®and Linden Lab™ are trademarks or registered trademarks of Linden Research, Inc.

This book is printed on acid-free paper.

CONTENTS

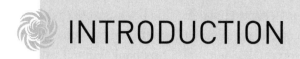

INTRODUCTION

WELCOME, BEWILDERED TRAVELER

Imagine coming upon a city that is a study in contrasts. On the one hand, it has a cosmopolitan population in the millions that's growing at a rate of about 20 percent a month, an embarrassment of oceanfront property, both private and commercial acreage of intriguing parks to rival the gardens of Paris, an impressive business district with towering office buildings, and opportunities for shopping and dining that would satisfy even those with the most discriminating tastes.

On the other hand, imagine that the city has a seedy side, with dank streets of darkly lit bars and clubs, and that surrounding this city are wooded areas in which are rumored to be nestled mysterious communities, some carrying out quasi-cultish rituals in the dead of night. Imagine also that, in this city, despite its millions of people, you find only tens of thousands of them out and about at any one time, with the lion's share of them not conducting business in the gleaming office towers or picnicking in the many parks, but roaming the winding streets of the seedy sector in search of ribald fun.

If this is the picture, the city you've come upon is Second Life, the online 3-D world launched in 2003—the one in which big-name companies like Toyota, H&R Block, and IBM have rushed to set up shop, marketing their wares and their services, with more companies following on their heels each week. This book is about why you should think about joining them with your own presence in this virtual world. If you do decide to join, this book will tell you how you should go about it, based on what these early adopters have learned. To judge by many news reports about Second Life, the reason you'd want to follow in the footsteps of the big players is money. The streets are paved with gold. Thanks to two pivotal innovations by the company that created the platform, Linden Lab in San Francisco, not only can you build your own presence in Second Life, as big and elaborate as you'd like, but you can do real business there as well. Since you retain ownership rights to what you build, you can engage in any form of commerce that makes sense to you (within applicable legal limits, of course) and exchange your proceeds for U.S. currency. What those glowing news reports tell you is that people are becoming millionaires.

The reality is more mundane, of course, and that's a good thing. Although some people are indeed reaping riches—there are some budding millionaires on the platform—and a lot of people are making *some* money, what the reality of the platform offers you is a measured opportunity to position your business in a very new way. This new way has little to do with the nature of the platform as you see it today—a strange experiment in free-market economics—but with the way analysts say you will see it tomorrow: as the new face of the Internet.

HOW TO MAKE
REAL MONEY
IN SECOND
LIFE

IF YOU HAVEN'T HEARD ABOUT **SECOND LIFE**, YOU WILL, SO WHAT'S IT ALL ABOUT?

In your quest to find business opportunity on the Internet, you always have to be on your guard against fads that are touted in the breathless prose of marketers as the *next big thing*. If left to the public relations professionals of the dot-com and other high-tech companies, we'd all be out of money as we chase the Web innovation that's going to change the way our customers and the people we want to be our customers do business.

Well, I'm here to tell you that the next big thing has indeed arrived, and it's time to get out your credit card, preferably your corporate card, and get on board. If you miss the train now, you'll have little opportunity to board later as the last car disappears around the bend.

I'm talking about Second Life, the virtual platform launched by San Francisco–based Linden Lab in 2003 to the acclaim of computer geeks around the world but to little notice by the rest of us.

What a difference a few years make. Second Life has become the darling of every mainstream news organization in the United States, with *BusinessWeek* describing the head of IBM as "gleeful" over it, *Fortune* giving it the best backhanded compliment it could think of by declaring it "not overhyped," *USA Today* touting it as the hot place for marketers today, and just about every business publication in the United States, including *Forbes,* the *Christian Science Monitor,* and *Information Week,* competing in a war of adjectives to describe it. And Reuters has assigned a correspondent to cover it full time.

For better or for worse, Second Life is exploding in popularity, and it's a good bet that most forward-looking companies will push themselves onto this platform and capitalize on it in any way they can. Many already have. This rush won't gather a full head of steam for years, and it might not even take place on Second Life at all but on an alternative platform that we've yet to hear about. But what the explosive growth in Second Life "residents" is showing us is that the days of virtual worlds as playgrounds primarily for computer geeks are quickly giving way to a different era as these kinds of platforms demonstrate their mass appeal.

That's surely bad news for the early adopters, those who joined Second Life for social networking rather than to tap into business opportunities, because with mass appeal comes mass marketing and all the transformative impact that has. But just as the World Wide Web was too useful for it to have remained an arcane communications network for researchers around the world, the virtual environment of a platform like Second Life is too compelling for it to remain the means by which a few computer geeks spend a lazy Sunday afternoon. The masses are coming, and they're bringing with them their ideas of what they want a virtual environment to be.

TIME TO HANG YOUR SHINGLE

At the risk of getting flamed in the blogs of a few early adopters of Second Life, the message of this book is that Second Life is for you—not just you, but for your business-building ideas, too. When you come to Second Life, don't come simply as someone looking for a novel way to spend a Sunday afternoon. Come as a person who's looking for ways to leverage what the analysts are calling a paradigm-breaking platform for marketing and, eventually, revenue growth.

Unlike other virtual platforms such as World of Warcraft, Second Life is not a game in any sense (although there's an important game aspect to it we talk about later) and was intended from its inception to be a neutral environment in which its residents could act out fully realized economic lives. This is what differentiates it from pure virtual networking environments like There.com, where teenagers congregate to socialize.

The opportunity within Second Life for users to experience a fully realized economic life is key, because while many early adopters brought a World of Warcraft mentality to Second Life, building fantasy worlds and engaging in role-playing, there's nothing in Second Life that predisposes the environment to take that shape. And indeed, the preponderance of places today in Second Life look far more like a suburban mall, right down to the asphalt parking lot, than a medieval castle

What's driving the construction of those parking lots is the prospect of making money, although not necessarily in what I

would call pure-play virtual businesses. As you'll read later, at least as the platform is currently constituted, pure-play virtual businesses are nearing, but not yet ready for, prime time, despite the emergence of many successful entrepreneurs on the Second Life platform. Your principal opportunities, rather, come from the platform's unique strength as a marketing bridge to your real-world business.

In Second Life, you're given a virtual alter ego, called an avatar, and a set of 3-D modeling tools to remake both your avatar and the environment in which your avatar lives. These tools are crucial because they enable you to be a creator of the environment, not just a resident of it. Without that set of tools—and equally crucially, without the right to own what you create, which Second Life grants you in the form of copyright and intellectual property rights—Second Life would be little more than a game without a plot.

Indeed, it was largely the decision by Linden Lab in late 2003 to throw out the playbook of other virtual environments and allow Second Life residents to retain ownership rights of their creations that lit the wick for the platform's astounding population growth. In mid-2007, its population was growing at a rate of close to 20 percent a month and nearing a population of 9 million residents.

By arming the platform's residents with the 3-D modeling tools and the rights of ownership, Linden Lab set the stage for avatars to live out genuine economic lives, with all the complexity that this entails. And that's what thousands are striving to do today, some succeeding more than others. But as today's roughly 9 million residents turn into 12 million in another few years, what today is an experiment in a parallel economy will turn into something much more important, as people start going to Second Life specifically to search for services, just as they now do on the Internet.

Corporations like Toyota and H&R Block are already treating Second Life like an economic laboratory, with Toyota showcasing its latest Scion and H&R Block its Tango line of tax preparation products. The train is still at the station, but its engines are running.

Despite the interest of the big guns like Toyota and H&R Block (Dell is there too, as you'd expect, along with a large vanguard of the Fortune 500), the environment is still in its infancy and the opportunity for you as an individual or as a representative of a small company or organization is wide open.

So, what form might your economic participation take? There are two ways to go: (1) It can be a conduit to your real-world business, much like your Web site is today, and (2) it can be a pure-play virtual business, although you can expect this to be a much more challenging road and something that I wouldn't bank on for another several years. I should add a third, and that's as a combination of both, and many businesses are doing that. We talk about all of these approaches in the pages that follow.

What I want to stress at the outset is that your foray into Second Life should be made professionally, at least if your intention is to tap your real-world expertise to make money. By "professionally" I mean you should work with a developer, just as you would for your Web site, and have a computer-assisted design specialist create your virtual presence rather than try to master the 3-D modeling tools yourself, even though those tools are there for anybody to use. Information on how to find these developers, how they work, and what they charge is provided in this book.

I make this suggestion because, although Linden Lab hands you the tools to be your own developer and much of what you see is indeed created by its residents, Second Life isn't a welcoming place for amateur builders. The geeks still rule the visual environment, so to speak. So while you can create your own presence, just as you can create your own Web site, it's easy to tell the professional from the amateur, and the amateur will not get the business.

Your role is to provide the ideas, the business plan, and the strategy to make your Second Life presence the go-to place for avatars. Wherever there are avatars, there are customers for you. It's my recommendation that you devote your energies to that rather than trying to master the design tools; by the time you master them, you will have lost valuable time you could have spent building your business.

WHAT KIND OF SHINGLE
SHOULD YOU HANG?

By the end of the first quarter of 2007, when the platform had about 7 million residents, almost 7,000 were earning up to $50 a month, and more than 150 were earning more than $5,000 a month. These numbers were increasing as of mid-2007. If Second Life were a game, these would be impressive numbers. But if you're thinking about making a serious economic foray onto this platform, they wouldn't look good to your accountant.

But the numbers show only the amount of virtual dollars, calculated in U.S.-dollar terms, exchanging hands in the virtual environment through what I'm calling pure-play virtual businesses: For example, I make a pair of virtual jeans for an avatar; I sell a pair of virtual jeans to an avatar. That kind of virtual commerce in the first quarter of 2007 totaled about $1.5 million a day, giving Second Life at that point a gross domestic product of about $550 million a year, or about the same as American Samoa in 2006.

What the numbers don't show is what Toyota and H&R Block are interested in: the boost to their business by using Second Life as a virtual platform to fuel their real-world businesses—not just in dollar terms (the platform is still so new that it could be years before any kind of return on investment is seen, at least for those making a major investment), but in marketing terms as measured by the amount of buzz a company generates.

"Firms are viewing this as where the Web was in 1994–1995," says Dave Levinson, a tech guru whose consulting company, Cranial Tap, in Round Hill, Virginia, works with companies moving into Second Life. I spoke with Levinson in mid-2007: "They're saying to themselves, 'This is potentially huge; we need to understand what it is, and how to leverage it.' Nobody is going in there with dollars signs in their eyes at this early stage. It's mostly about learning, about leveraging, and about understanding the community—what the community is doing, understanding its habits, what it likes, doesn't like—in preparation for where this space is likely going."

If you're looking at Second Life as an individual or as a representative of something other than a major corporation, you won't be in a position to invest big dollars in the hope of generating valuable buzz. The Toyota and H&R Block models wouldn't necessarily be for you. But just as the real-world economy has a place for all players, big and small alike, so does Second Life. With minimal investment and good strategic planning, you can create a bridge to your real-world business, attracting avatars to your virtual office and converting those avatars to visitors to your Web site.

That's what John Clayton was doing in early 2007. With little more than a few ads and some office space in Second Life, the Clearwater, Florida, real estate agent, who at the time was with Charles Rutenberg Realty, had seen traffic to a townhouse project he represented enjoy a boost. "The developer saw a big jump in traffic to its site," he told me.

Crucially, what makes Second Life more than just an unusual way to generate traffic to your Web site is its social aspect. A virtual world like Second Life is truly what a social Internet looks like.

You've probably heard the term quite a bit in the last year or two as businesses talk increasingly about it, but no Web site can be social in the way that a virtual environment can be.

In a 3-D virtual environment, potentially any number of avatars can congregate at a location at any one time. (Exactly how many would depend on server capacity.) They see one another, talk to one another, and can even lead one another around. In a case study you'll read more about later, one nonprofit organization in early 2007 was preparing to use Second Life as a platform for soldiers deployed in Iraq to meet their spouses or friends in real time in a mock USO setting to have dinner or go dancing. That's a true social Internet, a platform for genuinely compelling interactivity that's missing almost entirely from a Web site. Indeed, even on today's Internet, with all the video, audio, instant messaging, and glitzy graphics that are available, interaction is mostly solitary; you could be researching information, for example, and have no idea whether hundreds of others are researching the same information at the same time.

Why is that important? Suppose you're at a Second Life location looking at, say, information about a software product and another avatar at the site says he's used the product and invites you to pick his brain about it. Within minutes you've replicated the kind of interaction that previously you could have had only in person.

To be sure, there are elements on Internet sites that mimic that interaction: chat rooms, for one. But the kind of spontaneous conversations that get sparked in Second Life, and the way avatars travel around together from one location to another and engage in activity, put it in a category by itself.

For Clayton, Second Life amounted to little more than a highly unusual platform for marketing his real estate business. This kind of thing might be all you want. At the time, it worked for him. He spent little and achieved results, which is how a Web marketing effort ideally operates. When I last heard from him, he was exploring other uses of the platform. And that makes sense, because he's come a long way in learning how avatars use the environment and how to get his message in front of them. Thus, when people start using the platform more like the Internet, as many analysts contend will happen, he will be well positioned to leverage its growing popularity.

The bottom line is that with someone like Clayton, you have a person who's building his business virtually and employing his business prowess, just as he would in the real world. Although Clayton brings some computer design skills to his task, he could just as well have left the development to professionals, spending a minimal amount to present his business both professionally and effectively.

In the pages ahead, we look at different examples of the successful use of Second Life, both by individuals—a real estate professional, an attorney, an author—and by companies and organizations—an accounting firm, a consultancy, a nonprofit, a real estate brokerage, a clothing retailer. We'll look at their forays into Second Life from the perspective of their business strategy, and in so doing, we'll demystify the process so that you can look at Second Life with a clear vision of what you want to do and how you might do it.

THE BASICS,
OR WHY PEOPLE TAKE THEIR SECOND CHANCE ON SECOND LIFE SO SERIOUSLY

Before we get started, put yourself in your customer's place and pretend that you're a new resident of Second Life. You enter a world that is by turns strange and compelling—and in some ways not a little annoying. You arrive as an avatar—your virtual alter ego—and immediately you stumble about, walk into a fence, get lost in some bushes.

That, at least, is your experience if you're not 25 years old and a veteran of the canon of computer and Internet games known as "massively multiplayer role-playing games," or MMRPGs, that includes Ever-Quest and Star Wars Galaxies, games in which you play by manipulating an avatar through three-dimensional space. Certainly your children will take to Second Life more easily than you will, especially if they're already spending time on virtual sites like Entropia Universe, a fantasy platform, or There.com, the teen social networking site.

The amount of time it takes you to get comfortable with the controls for navigating this world isn't a minor matter. To the extent that a platform like Second Life becomes the new face of the Internet, it will depend in large part on how intuitive it is. Right now Linden Lab has its work cut out for itself. Depending on how adept you are at learning unfamiliar computer interfaces, it may take you hours of getting tangled up in bushes before you can comfortably move yourself around the environment, and moving yourself around the environment is as critical on this platform as is moving your curser around on the Internet. Indeed, your avatar is your cursor.

"Whatever its strengths are, at least right now there are lots of awkward things just in movement," says John Paul, CEO of the Dallas-based nonprofit consulting company AssociationWorks, which launched a Second Life presence in February 2007 and is starting to host virtual meetings for its clients.

This relatively high learning curve for many people is important to understand as you plan your foray into Second Life. Asking your customers, or the people you want to be your customers, to visit your setup on Second Life isn't the same as asking them to visit your Web site. There's a lot for them to do just to get onto the platform, let alone find their way to your site. The good news, though, is that things are getting simpler all the time. For example, avatars can now type in an exact address—what's known as a SLURL [a Second Life Uniform Resource Locator (URL)]—to get to exactly where they want to go. As intuitive as this appears, this hasn't always been possible. You'll read about this search capability later. But the bad news is that your customers still must make a commit-

ment of time and effort before you can count them as a valued visitor to your Second Life world. Even with the availability of SLURLs, your customers must have Second Life downloaded onto their computer and be account holders so that they can have an avatar, and they still need to know how to move that avatar around.

However, don't mistake these birth pangs of Second Life for the systemic shortcomings of an entire medium. Today, getting to and navigating this new terrain takes a little practice; tomorrow, it will be as second nature as holding a pencil, particularly if the barrier between the Internet and Second Life is taken down. Right now, Second Life is a world that exists on its own private browser. You can bounce back and forth between that world and the Internet only to the extent that a company or organization maintains a presence on both platforms, *and* you maintain an account on Second Life. Once those preconditions are eliminated, the 3-D virtual world will become a full-fledged extension of the Internet.

"Everyone will have an avatar in the future, just like today everyone has a PC," says Arlene Ciroula, COO of Baltimore-based accounting firm Katz, Abosch, Windesheim, Gershman & Freedman, P.A. (KAWG&F), which opened its virtual doors on Second Life in early 2007, making it one of the first accounting companies to do so. (H&R Block entered at around the same time.)

"You see a lot of parallels with the early stages of the Internet," says Levinson. "Fifteen years ago getting connected to the Web was difficult. We're seeing many of the same kinds of problems in Second Life today. It's data intensive, and its navigation is difficult if you're not used to it. But I see this as becoming the new Web and becoming easier to use just as the Web has."

HOW YOU GET TO THIS POINT

You start your virtual experience at Second Life's Web site, www. Secondlife.com, where you open an account and give your avatar a name that's fixed for the life of the account. The first name can be pretty much anything you want; the last name you choose from several dozen options. The account costs nothing, but if your goal is to position yourself professionally on the platform, you must open a premium account, which in mid-2007 cost $72 a year. What that buys you is an initial allocation of virtual money, weekly deposits into your account, and a homesteading option (an allocation of unimproved land that's yours for the taking if you want it), among other things.

It's important to note that the premium account also buys you credibility with others—not a small consideration in a world where people's real identities are behind a screen and avatars are known only by the assumed names they've been given. "Since anyone can come in for free and make a presence, people trust you a bit more if they've seen you've opened a premium account, because that signals that at a minimum you've given Linden Lab your credit card number," says Ciroula. "It shows you have something at stake."

The virtual money, denominated in what are called Linden dollars, is fully convertible to U.S. dollars at an exchange rate that, in mid-2007, was about 270 virtual dollars to $1. That exchange rate fluctuates daily, but throughout the first half of 2007 it stayed within a fairly narrow band, moving up or down by only a few percentage points. We talk about how Linden Lab regulates this market later, but it's important to keep in perspective the extreme difference in value between Linden dollars and U.S. dollars as you think about the ways to leverage Second Life for your business. At such a wide spread, the only reasonable way you can approach your in-world business is to act as if you were operating in a severely depressed economy. As Levinson puts it, "It's a thriving world, but if you're a car maker, don't expect to sell a virtual equivalent of your car for $3,000. That's not how you'll make your money."

The flip side of working in a depressed economy is low (real) costs. Although some companies are spending hundreds of thousands of dollars getting into the environment, many companies are getting into it professionally for as little as a few hundred dollars a year by relying on off-the-shelf, in-world design work (which they pay for in depressed, hyperinflated virtual dollars), an amount that wouldn't buy them a day's worth of labor by a professional Web designer. At that level of cost, it's almost too cheap not to establish a beachhead in Second Life. Of course, as the economy grows, so too will the value of the platform's currency. So expect the exchange rate to narrow in the years ahead. The watchword for you, then, is to understand that the cost of doing business in Second Life will grow along with its popularity, a very big reason for getting in early.

The Second Life Web site is also where you download the software that opens the door to the world on your desktop. That software is free, but since the quality of your virtual experience is determined by the capabilities of your computer, you'll need to pay to get your computer upgraded to handle the system if your graphics card isn't of a fairly recent vintage or if your storage capacity is limited. In its essence, Second Life is a data-heavy multimedia 3-D Internet world, so it requires fairly robust graphics capabilities and plenty of memory. Expect to pay from $70 to $225 if you need upgraded components, and another $200 if you hire someone to handle the installation.

What you get with your upgrades is the ability to fully render the 3-D world. Visually, the investment in upgrades is rewarding because, if it's nothing else, Second Life is a feast for the eyes, in a league with the graphics in most computer games, including visually rich games like EverQuest and World of Warcraft, although MMRPG aficionados swear it falls short of those games' visual quality. It's in part because of this visual richness that the platform not infrequently suffers from what's called lag: delayed downloading time, not unlike delayed downloading of some multimedia-heavy Web sites. But as we discuss later, although this lag can be a factor as you plan your Second Life strategy, ultimately it's a solvable problem. Much like the platform's clunky navigation, it's what must be seen today as a tactical problem rather than a strategic one.

"Competition [among virtual platforms] at some point will be great, and I would think the next iteration of this will be very different in terms of speed," John Paul told me.

Your entry into the Second Life world is via an island. Although it isn't by air, the unfamiliarity can make your arrival feel a bit like a soldier parachuted into enemy territory. Navigating your avatar around a 3-D world is anything but intuitive, and, as with learning to drive, no amount of instruction beforehand is equal to getting behind the controls and piloting yourself around. This is why you might spend quite a bit of time trying to disentangle yourself from the bushes.

You're provided two sets of controls, one for manipulating your avatar (which includes the ability to fly as well as to walk and run) and one for manipulating what you see. It's this latter set of controls you're likely to find a challenge to master. And the reason is simple: While we have experience moving an object through space, whether it's ourselves, a tricycle, a bicycle, or a car, few of us have experience changing our orientation in space, but that's the objective of this second set of tools, known as the *camera controls*.

The camera controls enable you to park your avatar and peer around the environment stealthily, looking around corners and seeing what's behind you. They enable you to look at yourself from above or from the perspective of another avatar. It's a little disconcerting at first and even a bit creepy, but the camera controls are for more than spying around your environment. Camera controls make it possible for you to use the set of modeling tools you're given for building objects in 3-D space. The ability to peer at your object from far and near, above and behind, enables you to control what you're building.

What might be called a third set of controls is your search and "teleporting" dashboard. Second Life comes with a search engine along the lines of Google or Yahoo! so you can "teleport" directly to sites based on search criteria you enter. You can conduct searches in which results are listed hierarchically, based on their popularity as measured by their recent traffic count, or you can conduct searches under a paid classified tab in which results are based on sites' advertising expenditures.

Thanks to the new SLURL addresses, as long as you have Second Life open on your computer, you can bypass this search function entirely and go to a location directly from the World Wide Web by typing the site's coordinates into your browser, just as you do a URL. In the view of some analysts, the SLURL system represents a huge improvement if your aim is to create a pathway between your Web site and your Second Life space, because it enables you to give out your virtual address just as you would your URL.

"Before this, there wasn't an easy URL that your browser could use to go directly to a spot in Second Life," says Storm Williams, strategic director for marketing consulting firm MojoZoo in Winston-Salem, North Carolina. "With the development of SLURL, Linden came out with a way to build URLs that you could put in your Web page to go directly to *xyz* coordinates. That was a major step."

WHAT DO YOU NEED TO KNOW, AND WHY DO YOU NEED TO KNOW IT?

To be sure, if your objective is to leverage Second Life in the same way that you're leveraging the Web, then all this talk about appearing on an island, learning to master movement controls, building objects in 3-D, and coming to understand the different search functions is really beside the point. You don't need to master any of these "play" aspects of the Second Life platform to chart your strategic course, just as you don't need to master programming and design to operate an effective Web site. There are professionals who can handle the nitty-gritty for you.

But just as you can't effectively chart your strategic course on the Internet without a firsthand knowledge of it—what's on the Web, how people use it, how it's evolving—you can't plausibly come to understand how to leverage your Second Life presence without coming to know it. What makes sense in a three-dimensional social platform like Second Life is unique and doesn't provide a good fit for a transplant of your Web strategy. So spending time on the ground is a must.

"The typical client we go to isn't clear about Second Life," says Williams, the marketing consultant. "You have to show them. Once you show them, then they get it. But when you're just describing it, it's like describing the Web to somebody that's never heard the term 'Internet' and has no idea what it is beyond their conceptualizing ability. When they see it, then they get it: 'Oh, that's what you're talking about. I got you.'"

That said, although you can't spend too much time coming to understand the rhythms of the world, it makes little sense to invest more time than is necessary learning how to build things. Although building objects is a central aspect of Second Life—the environment in which your avatar lives is almost entirely the product of other avatars and professional developers, not Linden Lab—you don't need to build anything. Everything an avatar could possibly want, from clothes, to furniture, to buildings, to animals, to neighborhoods, to cities, to parks, is already built and more is being built daily. And if you can't find what you need, there are plenty of professionals available to handle your development project.

It's this robust construction activity by the platform's armies of residents and professional developers that makes it possible for individuals or small companies to get set up with such a small initial investment. Ciroula's accounting company, for example, launched its presence in Second Life in early 2007 for just a few hundred dollars, in large part because it was able to acquire most of what it needed to outfit and operate a virtual office using off-the-shelf, resident-made products. These are products whose costs are denominated in Second Life's highly depressed virtual dollars.

"My IT director and I had gone out and purchased various pieces of inventory, like a desk, chairs, and pictures for our office," says Ciroula. "I had met some folks on Second Life, and one of them had a small piece of land available that we leased. Our landlord put a building on it for me, and from there I went out and bought the inventory for our space." The total out of pocket costs amounted to less than $100 a month.

Even a technology powerhouse like IBM, which in mid-2007 had about a dozen islands in Second Life (each island a 16-acre "sim" of land), had in at least one case gone shopping for what it needed to get a client onto the platform at very little cost rather than have its own programmers build something from scratch. "On one of the islands that IBM put up, for a consumer electronics retailer, the facility was entirely prefab," says Bill Nissim, president of a marketing consulting company in the Los Angeles area, called ibranz, that in mid-2007 was helping businesses get set up virtually. "They just went out and got [an entire building complex] that cost them something like $20 or $30."

To be sure, IBM fleshed out that facility with intricate custom development work, investing heavily in programming to create unique, state-of-the-art functionality on the inside of the facility, thereby making it a showcase destination. And the company on the whole is set to invest some $10 million over time in Second Life as well as some other virtual platforms. But the example shows that even in high-end 3-D design work, much of the existing inventory by Second Life residents is of a quality to attract even a company like IBM, and the cost scale—at least during this early period in the platform's evolution—can't be beat.

Indeed, with the resident-built inventory there's really no parallel to the Internet. That's why entrepreneurs can open their doors for literally pennies. A nutritionist who in mid-2007 went by the name of DietAdvisor Vella on Second Life launched a pure-play virtual nutrition consulting business for a handful of dollars, leasing an existing office and acquiring a desk, a computer, and a few chairs, to give her office a professional look.

"I just bought everything I needed, spending less than $10," says Vella, who asked to be referenced by her virtual identity. "I've never owned a business before. Now I'm planning on starting one, and this helps me with it." Her trade takes place entirely on the virtual platform, with pricing based on Linden dollars (one of her consultations at the time cost 1,200 Lindens), so although the diet advice she's dispensing is for the real people behind the avatars, the in-world business contains no links outside Second Life and so is a pure-play virtual business that, for all practical matters, cost her only her time—an eight-hour investment—to get going. A virtual steal.

In a similar way, corporate performance consultant Mark Friedman spent just a handful of dollars to set up a modest facility on Second Life and to post an advertisement for his book, *Trying Hard Is Not Good Enough*, which details his consulting principles. He bought a small parcel of land for which he's paying about $5 a month in tier fees (basically, an ownership tax, about which you'll read more later). He built all the structures himself, so beyond an investment of about 20 hours of his time, he was able to outfit his site with a gathering room, some benches, landscaping, and the ad for his book for essentially nothing. "It helps if you're good with graphic arts and computer programming, because both of those skills come in handy [if you don't want to pay someone else to do it]," says Friedman. "In some ways it's easy to develop objects, but in other ways, to do anything sophisticated takes a lot of work."

Although a big poster of his book is the first thing visiting avatars see when they arrive at his site, increasing book sales is secondary to his aims for his space, which he's turning into a virtual "public square" for business consultants who use the practices presented in the book. "I'm trying to give people a place where they can come to [exchange best practices on the training methods on which the book is based] and interact with other people who are doing the work," he says.

SEPARATING YOURSELF
FROM YOUR AVATAR

Vella's business is typical of the pure-play model, and it illustrates the point about both the strength and the weakness of today's virtual environment as a business platform: Because the economy is extremely depressed, it can be virtually cost-free to get in. But by the same token, the returns delivered are mostly in micro amounts. That's why your best bet today is to use Second Life as a bridge to your real-world business, as Friedman is doing. Your costs are in highly depressed Linden dollars, but your returns are in U.S. dollars. Later you'll meet a lawyer who, like Ciroula, spent nominal amounts getting established virtually, and within a short period of time generated more than $7,000 in billable hours from two clients he met on the platform. It's like developing a product in a low-wage country for sale at prices set in a high-wage country.

That's not to say that businesspeople aren't making money in pure-play operations. By now you've likely heard of Second Life's most famous resident, Anshe Chung, or, if you haven't, you probably will. She's been on CNN and in *Fortune, Der Spiegel*, and the *Financial Times*, among other business publications, and made the June 2004 cover of *BusinessWeek*. Chung is the in-world alter ego of Ailin Graef, a Chinese entrepreneur who lives in Germany and is one of Second Life's first business barons, generating more than $1 million in 2006 based mainly on the business of buying and selling virtual land on the platform. Her success has been so dazzling that in early 2007 a German venture capital firm, European Founders Fund, bought a 10 percent stake in her business.

There are thousands of sims of land in Second Life. Chung isn't close to cornering the real estate market there, but there's no question she's got her sights set on the big picture. As of mid-2007, she was reported to hold hundreds of sims of land, and her purely virtual property transactions had netted her a big enough cash hoard that she was able to finance a move into real-world commercial real estate. Meanwhile, she maintains her virtual real estate business, employing a team of avatars to keep the transactions flowing.

Another entrepreneur, a designer named Veronica Brown, made a reported $60,000 in 2006 from sales of her clothing line. Not counting her time, a good chunk of her income might very well be profit, to the extent her costs are denominated in Linden dollars.

In all, some 1,500 people were earning at least $500 a month in pure-play virtual businesses in the first quarter of 2007, according to economic figures tracked by Linden Lab, and more than 600 people were earning at least $1,000 a month. You will see these numbers grow. If the platform was generating $1.5 million in daily transaction volume in that quarter, when there were just under 6 million residents, and if the population grows at the rate of, say, 3,000 a day (a reasonable estimate given its roughly 20 percent monthly growth rate), then in a few years' time, when the population doubles to 12 million, you can expect transaction volume to rise to at least $3 million a day, generating an annual GDP of more than $1 billion. This would be more than the GDP of Saint Lucia in 2006.

But by the time that happens, Second Life will be a very different place: far more commercialized, certainly, and also far less depressed. The currencies of growing economies stabilize. No one can predict what the exchange rate will be two years from today, but you can bet it won't be 270:1, even if Linden Lab allows it to float within only a relatively narrow band. The cost of doing business will go up, almost certainly not enough to have more than a minimal impact on your in-world marketing plans for your real-world businesses. But very possibly it could dampen somewhat any pure-play virtual business you'd like to operate. That said, although your costs will rise, so too will your revenue as your prices rise in tandem. But you'll face start-up costs that will be that much higher, and it's not clear that people will be willing to pay higher prices for in-world services.

For now, pure-play virtual businesses, despite the Chungs and the Browns of the world, remain the domain of hobbyists like Diet-Advisor Vella, spending her $10 and earning in exchange her fees of 1,200 Lindens (about $4) per consultation.

That puts the focus on what most businesses today are doing in Second Life, which is launching a presence solely to get their real-world business before an audience of roughly 9 million highly engaged consumers, currently mostly men and, maybe surprisingly, currently mostly outside the United States. Reports based on self-selected surveys indicate current membership at about 60 percent outside the United States, a good chunk of that from Europe, mainly the United Kingdom. Indeed, both the European Union and the Swedish government in mid-2007 were contemplating setting up virtual embassies on the platform.

In age, residents almost surely skew older than your typical gamers but younger than your typical buyers of life insurance and individual retirement accounts (IRAs). What's important, at least to the marketing pros swarming over Second Life to study its potential, is that the audience is highly engaged with the medium, meaning that it's hyper aware of what's happening on the platform, who's coming in, who's expanding, where the neat things are. This is stated in contrast to radio and television audiences, who marketers say are increasingly tuning out those media, indeed, using the media more as background noise to which attention is only occasionally paid.

"People are swamping the servers to get in Second Life, says Williams, the MojoZoo executive. "No one's really seen it before. That makes it exciting and that why it's a good place for people to advertise their real-world products in."

With this as background, let's take a look at some first principles for building your virtual presence.

AVOIDING THE THIRD RAIL OF SECOND LIFE: **FIRST STEPS**

I f your objective is to tap this new medium to boost your brand, there are eight rules of thumb to consider following before you take your first step. These rules, which I call "Avoiding the third rail of Second Life: first steps," were culled from interviews with a dozen businesspeople who've jumped onto the platform and have developed a sense of what you can and can't do to make yours a welcomed presence. What I'm calling the third rail of Second Life is the protocol that governs so many popular social Internet interfaces. This is in the early stages of their evolution, so don't expect too much. Just have fun.

DON'T EXPECT TOO MUCH

1. Match Your Ambition to the System's Capacity

Second Life's frustrating problem with "lag," the delayed downloading time you experience when you enter, is only one facet of a larger problem: grid capacity.

Not that long ago, Linden Lab was operating on about 2,000 servers, which at the time was accommodating a resident population of about 3.5 million. Up until that point, and since then, the number of servers has been in constant flux. By some estimates, Linden is adding servers at the rate of dozens a week. What the company is learning is that its server capacity is struggling to accommodate the popularity of its platform. Although the company continues to boost its server capacity and to make improvements in other ways, and there are tech professionals confident that Linden's grid issues are eminently solvable, the reality is that each sim today can accommodate only a certain amount of traffic at a time, particularly if the area is highly built up, containing a lot of complex programming. Thus, depending on where your site is, and whether it's located in an older part of the grid or a newer part, you can host only between 40 and 100 avatars on a 16-acre plot at a time. (And some techies estimate that Second Life's capacity, as it stands today, will max out at 100,000 simultaneous visitors, no matter how widely avatars are spread out along the grid.)

Clearly, even on a higher-capacity server you're not going to get as much traffic as you would at a company brown bag luncheon. But keep this capacity issue in perspective. Would you even want to have more than 100 avatars on your site at one time, even if you could? It's important to keep in mind that, although a virtual platform like Second Life is in some quarters touted as the next generation of the Web, it remains a three-dimensional space that, were it to have unlimited grid capacity, can physically accommodate only so many virtual bodies in a virtual room at one time. In this sense, a virtual room is no different from a real room. Even a real-world mega business like, say, Microsoft, can't get more than a few dozen people into a standard sized conference room in its Redmond headquarters for a presentation at one time. Outside of a big, one-off spectacle like a product launch or a company convention, it's not that common for any real-world business to host large numbers of people at any one time. Far more common are small-scale gatherings, and for these types of events the current Second Life capacity is adequate. At the same time, even as Second Life evolves and it (or another virtual platform) assumes a greater Web-like presence, the World Wide Web will continue to coexist and absorb the large traffic demands of mass numbers of people searching for information and consuming products and services. Criticisms of Second Life about its grid capacity (and the criticism is out there) is constructive, but surely the problem can't be looked at outside the context of the same space capacity problems that bedevil business in real life. This kind of criticism is like saying that the business model for a national shoe store chain doesn't work because each of its stores on average can reasonably accommodate only 35 customers looking for shoes at one time.

In any case, even today it's possible to accommodate a few hundred people on Second Life with a little ingenuity. Some companies are hosting events at sites that sit at the crossroads of four separate servers, enabling them in effect to tap the processing power of all four servers for a single event. And in some cases Linden Lab can take steps to boost processing power to a server if it knows ahead of time that you want to do something big.

That said, if Second Life fails to live up to its potential in the years ahead, there's no doubt that grid capacity will be a major reason. In the interest of fully airing these concerns, I direct you to a short article, "The Phony Economics of Second Life," from the U.K. publication *The Register*. As the title implies, it's written from the point of view of someone who's not smitten by Second Life. You'll find the URL for the online version of the article in the notes section in the back of the book.

2. Remember That Most Avatars Today Are Still Just Playing a Game

Businesspeople are jumping into Second Life at a breakneck pace, and each day another press release is sent to reporters trumpeting the fact that this company or that company now has a presence there. This interest makes perfect sense because, whatever growing pangs the platform is experiencing, there's no question that businesses now have an opportunity to test entirely new types of business models there. Who wouldn't want to be one of the first in the space?

But in the midst of this hype it's helpful to remember that, in the end, the most frequent visitors to Second Life are people just playing a game, albeit a game without formal rules and that takes different forms depending on who's playing. What becomes clear to anyone who spends a bit of time on the platform is that the principal game is a kind of dating game that typically begins at a club or a beach. Avatars tend to congregate in places with high concentrations of other avatars, and these are the clubs and the beaches. At these places, avatars seek to get to know one another and then extend formal offers of "friendship" to one another. I put friendship in quotes becomes it's an orchestrated process in which one avatar grants the other permission to teleport the avatar around. It's a little like exchanging phone numbers or e-mail addresses. It signifies a certain level of seriousness. The next stage of the game involves different ways to deepen the relationship, possibly leading to some type of consummation, which can take any number of forms.

Thus, dating is arguably one of the main games people play. There are other games, and indeed, a good chunk of the early space was built for highly formalized role-playing. For that reason, a substantial portion of the Second Life world continues to be about things like Gorean fantasy life, dungeons, and magical waterfalls. (If you're not familiar with Gorean fantasy life, it has to do with a set of rules of social hierarchy based on the science fiction novels of John Norman, a follower of Edgar Rice Burroughs.)

It's useful to note that much of the pure-play virtual businesses that have been sustained over time cater in one form or another to these dating and role-playing games. To be successful at the dating game, for example, your avatar must look good. As a result, there's robust commercial activity in the making, buying, and selling of attractive skins (customized bodies and faces), clothing, and jewelry. As the new friends spend time on the platform together, they need places to go and things to do. To accommodate that, there's robust trade in objects that avatars give to one another as gifts (glasses of wine, flowers, cigars) and cozy places to which avatars like to retreat, some of which cost money. You can rent a hotel room, for example.

Thus, you have what you might consider parallel universes in Second Life: a kind of city-chic dating scene and dungeon and dragons role-playing coexisting with an increasingly hyper commercial world of office complexes that wouldn't look out of place near Fort Lauderdale. The two worlds don't often intersect, and if your ultimate aim is to send traffic from your Web site to your 3-D Second Life presence, the two won't necessarily need to intersect. But these parallel universes are part of the richness of the platform, and certainly what I've described is simply the two poles of a continuum that contains every type of environment in between. So you've got shopping complexes and office parks that, as hard as it might be to imagine, manage to straddle both worlds, the fantasy and the mundane, although some do so more successfully than others.

Given these parallel environments, you need to be clear on two objectives up front: (1) who you want your audience to be, and (2) how you want to maintain a harmonious coexistence with Second Life users whose objectives are very different from yours.

Establishing these objectives will determine many of your tactical moves: where you locate your site, what it's going to look like, what kinds of activities you'll host, and how you're going to market your services or products. It'll also determine what you won't do: where you won't market your services, where you won't go around canvassing for business, and how you won't present yourself in certain environments or when interacting with certain avatars.

All this said, even role-playing avatars are people, too, and any person who spends a lot of time in Second Life enjoying its game aspects is surely a good candidate for your business, because as long as someone is present in the world for hours on end, that person might as well look for an attorney just in case he might need one. That's how Stevan Lieberman, the attorney based in Washington, D.C., found one of his clients. A specialist in patent law, Lieberman, who sometimes goes around Second Life as an orange triceratops, got to talking to another avatar who turned out to be a software developer. Eventually they entered into an agreement for Lieberman to provide some legal work. "You just get to networking with people at random," says Lieberman. "You never know who you're going to run into."

3. You Can't Escape Taxes, Even in Second Life

It's true that the U.S. government isn't taxing the Linden dollars you earn in Second Life, although it certainly can tax your virtual income once you pull it off the platform and convert it to U.S. dollars. Whether you'll attract an audit for stating on your Form 1040 that your income was generated virtually, I can't say. However, there's a book I can refer you to on that topic, called *Play Money: How I Quit My Day Job and Made Millions Trading Virtual Loot* (Basic Books: 2006), by Julian Dibbell. I've also reproduced an article of Dibbell's on the topic from a 2006 issue of *Legal Times*, called "Dragon Slayers or Tax Evaders?" You'll find that reproduced in whole later in the book.

Taxation of virtual commerce is an evolving issue, so who knows? Tomorrow the federal government might actually not wait until you convert your Lindens to dollars. "Right now we're at the preliminary stages of looking at the issue [of taxing virtual income] and what kind of public policy questions virtual economies raise—taxes, barter exchanges, property, and wealth," says Dan Miller, an economist with the Joint Economic Committee in the U.S. Congress. The quote is from a late 2006 Reuters piece, and as of mid-2007, the committee had yet to release any paper on the issue.

What I can say is that Linden Lab needs to make money from its platform somehow, and one way it does that, beyond the $72 it takes in annually from each of its premium account holders, is to levy what it calls a *monthly tier fee* on property owners. The fee in mid-2007 ranged from $5 to $195 based on the amount of land owned, calculated in square meters. Those fees are calculated in dollars, not Lindens, so if you own an entire island, or about 65,500 square meters, you're looking at close to $2,000 a year in levies, and if you own two islands or more, which you might want to do if you're trying to create a whole world, as some developers are doing, you're talking $4,000 and up. Now you're getting into real money, although for most small businesses, owning an entire island would certainly be an extravagance. If your purpose is to establish an office from which to send people to your Web site, you can probably do that by leasing improved space from a landowner, with the lease amount based in part on the desirability of the location and the quality of the building, just as it is in real life. If you're leasing space, it's your landlord who's paying the tier fee, not you.

DON'T TAKE AWAY THE FUN

4. People Are Looking for Things to Do

Although Second Life from its inception was to be a neutral platform on which people could carry out fully realized virtual lives, economic and otherwise, there remains an unmistakable game quality to the environment, and you ignore this at your peril. In addition to the role-playing sites, there are any number of locations designed specifically to host games, including county fair types like bean bag tosses. Indeed, before Linden Lab put the brakes on in-world gambling operations in mid-2007 (in response to complicated legal jurisdictional rules), casino-type operations were contributing some 15 percent to the platform's gross domestic product (GDP).

On the one hand, in-world games are pure-play virtual businesses using sophisticated programming to simulate real-world play experiences. But on the other hand, in-world games speak to one of the fundamental tenets of attracting avatars to your site and keeping them there: *having things to do*. In this respect, avatars are little different from the people who are directing their movements. Avatars have arms, legs, and eyes, and the "game" of Second Life involves finding novel ways to deploy those arms, legs, and eyes; otherwise you might as well surf the platform with a cursor. Therefore, the more interactive features you offer at your site, the easier it is for you to lure traffic to it and to keep the traffic there.

"To have a place that just takes after the Web [as an information source without interactive features] doesn't leverage the environment," says Levinson of Cranial Tap. "The real win is having people interested in what you're doing in your space. People want to hang out."

Indeed, it's this desire for people to have their avatars interacting in some way that makes the platform's role-playing aspect so compelling and undoubtedly accounts for the continued popularity of the platforms' fantasy worlds. That certainly doesn't mean that you want to make role-playing a feature of customers' experience at your site, although if you built a role-playing component into the experience, that would be one unmistakable way of fully leveraging the uniqueness of the virtual platform. But it does mean that you shouldn't consider your site complete if doesn't have anything for avatars to do once they're there. If this is a problem, it's an easy one to solve if you're a company like Toyota. At its site your avatar can hop into a Scion and go for a test drive. You can't get more interactive than that.

Mercedes Benz has launched a similar site, with a race track at which avatars can suit up in a racing outfit and helmet and take a car out for a spin. The site also hosts a band at certain times. "It's immersive," says Storm Williams. "They've really gone to great lengths to figure out what Second Life is all about and how to interface with it." Pontiac also has a big site for driving.

Dell's site is focused on interactivity, too, as you'd expect from the company that not too long ago was selling more PCs than anyone else in the world. (Hewlett-Packard is now the leader.) At its island, you can hop onto a jelly bean–shaped pod for a ride to its computer factory, where you can sit down at a design table to pick and choose components you want for your computer and order them right there. In effect, you're acting as the computer technician who's building her own computer. It's a game, but it's also real, because after you build your computer, you can actually buy it if you want to.

Ideas for interactivity are less obvious for companies offering abstract services such as accounting, but companies are finding creative solutions all the same. When it launched its Second Life site in late March 2007, national residential real estate brokerage Coldwell Banker created a computer-driven golden retriever to greet visitors and take them where they want to go based on what they're looking for, whether it's virtual or real-world home listings or virtual or real-world mortgage information. The dog is modeled on the "personal retriever" that's on the company's Web site and featured in some of its advertising, so in addition to the interactivity, the company's getting strong brand leverage by keeping the virtual site well integrated with the company's marketing in other media. The company's Second Life space also maintains a museum gallery with interactive exhibits in which avatars can walk through major U.S. events of the last 100 years, a tactical way for the company to tout its 100-year anniversary, which it reached in 2006.

What the Toyota and Coldwell Banker examples share are big dollar signs. Clearly neither company went on a shopping excursion in Second Life to find off-the-shelf programming to create what are highly complex animations and objects, at least for some of their sites' features. Rather, they likely had some custom-made applications created to give visitors state-of-the-art experiences. But interactivity and high costs don't have to go together. You can find off-the-shelf animations and other types of interactive features for your site. Obviously these won't be as sophisticated as what I've just described. You might simply have an interactive laptop on a desk that sends avatars to various features around your site, but this is more than enough to give visitors a reason to "hang out," as Levinson put it.

5. When Your Main Sense Is Sight, Appearance Is Everything

Although Second Life is a multimedia platform that provides an experience for your eyes as well as your ears (in-world voice became available in mid-2007), it is primarily a visual platform and you consume it through your eyes. What this means is that places, like avatars, are judged immediately and without forgiveness by how they look. It's for this reason that avatars wandering aimlessly into, say, a Gorean fantasy world are sent a message that says, in no uncertain terms, that they're expected to play an appropriate part if they want to stay in the realm and, what's more, they can be asked to leave if they don't fit in visually.

In a role-playing world such a rule about appearance makes perfect sense, because wandering through a dark, forbidding forest in cuffed jeans and a T-shirt, like a character out of *West Side Story*, works against the nature of role-playing, which relies on the suspension of reality to be successful. But residents place a premium on appearance throughout Second Life, not just in the role-playing areas. It a sense, appearance is all that residents have to go on, since avatars can keep their identities cloaked if they want, revealing only what they want and being coy about whether what they reveal is true or false. Given this, if avatars were books, you really can judge them only by their cover, at least until relationships are established and some bonds of trust are forged.

This focus on appearance, along with the itch to be doing something, engaging in some activity, is no doubt what lies behind the appeal of shopping as an in-world activity. At any given time there might be 30,000 avatars active on the platform, and you can bet at least a quarter of them are out shopping, most likely for clothes. There are probably as many clothing stores per 16 acres in Second Life as on Chicago's Miracle Mile or New York's Fifth Avenue. And I'm guessing that much of the $1.5 million in daily dollars changing hands on the platform in the first quarter of 2007 was for clothes.

What this preoccupation with appearance tells you is that your in-world location will rise or fall based not just on what it offers avatars to do but how it looks. Time is too short and the options too numerous for avatars to waste time on a site that isn't visually appealing to them. For that reason those who develop on the platform, whether as an individual doing a small-scale project for fun or a Fortune 500 company going all out to make Second Life a major bridge to its real-world business, pay much time and attention to making the environment intriguing, what you might call affectively rich or atmospheric. This is important because it changes what you would ordinarily consider acceptable for you or your business. Remember the fact that Stevan Lieberman, the Washington patent attorney, goes around as an orange triceratops when he's in-world. That's not to say your office, if you're an attorney, should be constructed in a tree house or a cave; however, it is to say that you can construct your office in a tree house or a cave, and you wouldn't be straying outside the conventions of what is and isn't acceptable in Second Life.

Any business that has real-world brand equity to protect, like the accounting firm KAWG&F, would be taking a risk if it set up shop in a tree house. At the same time, for it to set up shop in an entirely conventional context, giving no nod whatsoever to the uniqueness of the virtual platform, would be to miss the point of the platform and, what's more, would be violating one of the big unwritten rules of Second Life: appearances matter.

For most companies, the approach KAWG&F has taken makes sense, because, as you'll see later, it strikes a visual balance between the extreme and the banal, intriguing enough to survive the judgment of appearance-obsessed residents on the one hand and conventional enough to maintain its hard-won real-world brand equity on the other.

6. You Can't Get Around It:
Second Life Has a Robust Adult Life

Just as on the World Wide Web, where the sacred and the profane coexist in sometimes uneasy proximity to each other, any foray you make into Second Life must be done with the understanding that adult interaction is a part of what goes on in-world, at least in certain areas. Thus you need to decide up front what part of the world you want to occupy, PG or R (mature). The easy approach is to build your presence in a PG location and limit your advertising to searches that default to PG-only sites. But in doing that, you're almost certainly limiting your reach, since the lion's share of traffic occurs in mature areas, and moreover there are plenty of strategies at your disposal to keep adult activities at bay when you're in a mature area.

First, although most regions in Second Life are designated mature, that designation alone doesn't mean the presence of adult activity (really, we're talking about adult businesses, like provocative clothing stores, and adult behavior, like nudity or sex, in which avatars go on autopilot through preprogrammed animations to simulate intimate acts); it means only that adult activity isn't prohibited. The mature designation, in other words, isn't a synonym for a red-light district, and in fact, the vast majority of sites in mature regions are not adult-oriented. Thus, you can locate your office complex in a mature region and feel reasonably confident that the likelihood of any adult behavior happening on the site is small— no more likely than at a real-world complex, where anyone, if you think about it, is free to commune with nature as long as he's willing to pay the consequences should he get caught.

Second, there are steps you can take to limit inappropriate behavior. Among these are automated messages greeting avatars upon their arrival and setting out your conditions for allowing them onto your property. Whether you would want to take a heavy-handed approach like this is a call only you can make, and it might be something you do only if you face a recurring problem. But that and other steps like it are among the tools at your disposal. You have tools for enforcement, too, including working with private in-world security firms, which can help you track visitors.

The question for you, then, is wouldn't it be easier to locate in a PG area? It would be, except that being in a PG area is no guarantee that rogue avatars won't, say, go streaking on your site. If they do, you have the option of communicating the violation to Linden Lab, which can impose restrictions on people's accounts if the company determines that the violation constitutes a breach of its terms of agreement for residents. What you don't get in a PG area are two benefits that come with locating in a mature area: one, the spillover traffic from nearby popular hotspots, like clubs and beaches, which are mostly in mature areas, and two, with less random traffic, strong positioning in the in-world search engine, because the regular (i.e., nonpaid) search results are based on popularity.

To be sure, as the population base of Second Life grows and its demographic profile shifts farther away from the thirty-something male gamers who made up a good part of its initial population, the PG areas will become more competitive with the mature areas, their content becoming more robust, and the tactical benefits of locating in mature areas will wane. But for now, the sacred and the profane coexist, and that's a matter you'll want to take into account.

7. "Griefing" Happens, Too;
It's Another Thing You Can't Avoid

Given its attraction initially to gamers and others who fancy themselves outlaws in the Wild West of the Internet, Second Life is rich
in mischief, or "griefing," although probably not as much as the
mischief makers would like you to believe. Of course, there are sto-
ried moments of noble mischief making in times past, like the
assault with inappropriate objects on Anshe Chung's press conference showcasing her financial success. The intrusion of objects,
some projectile-like in nature, became so heavy that Chung was
forced to reconvene her conference in a more secure location.

Clearly, mischief making of that nature is generally harmless,
more annoying than anything else, even entertaining in the view
of some. And in its defense it should be viewed as part of the mosaic of experiences the platform provides. However, there are steps
you can take to exercise levels of control against such intrusions.
First, you can create borders that make your land accessible to
avatars only with your permission. The way the permission process
works is typically through a membership arrangement.

It goes without saying that, if your goal is to attract as much
traffic to your site as possible, erecting a barrier is an extreme
measure. Although I'm not a tech specialist myself, my guess is
that even these barriers can ultimately be breached by mischief
makers who know how to stay one step ahead of tough information
technology (IT) security.

Second, griefing isn't widely supported, and, what's more, it will
become rarer as the population continues its shift away from its
gamer roots and becomes more representative of the population as
a whole. Really, most people just want their avatars to go shopping.

Other types of mischief will be more familiar to you, since
they're hardly unique to a virtual platform. I'm talking about the
same kind of mischief you can't get away from even in a sleepy sub-
urb: people behaving badly. Public displays of nudity are one thing;
avatars packing heat are another. Yes, there are guns in Second

Life. But, unlike in real life, the guns are only annoying, not dangerous. It's not uncommon to be greeted with a message as you drop into some locations that says, "No guns allowed." Do these messages make a difference? Probably as much as they do when asking avatars to keep their clothes on—meaning not much.

What you can do is work with an in-world security firm to put security measures in place and also track who comes to and goes from your property. That way repeated offenders can be contacted and, perhaps in some cases, their accounts restricted by Linden Lab. Just search "security" in the in-world search engine and pay some of the companies a visit.

8. This Could All End Tomorrow

Unlike our real-world economy, where systems and institutions have been set up to provide investors with a measure of protection against acts of nature and other unexpected disruptions to markets, Second Life is merely the online world of a private company that could go belly up at any time. The companies that invest hundreds of thousands of dollars in Second Life are clearly banking that bankruptcy isn't in Linden Lab's future, and I'm sure they take heart in the fact that some pretty big names in the world of the Internet, like Amazon's Jeff Bezos and Lotus's Mitch Kapor, are financial backers of Linden Lab. But you never know.

What's clear, though, is that the trajectory of a platform like Second Life is bigger than the company that spawned it. There are other virtual worlds, and there are more to come. Although the Linden Lab servers might shut down someday, the huge investment in virtual development won't shut down along with them; another company will have every incentive to power up those severs again so that the avatars in Second Life can continue to live their virtual lives, maybe as part of another platform, but living and breathing (well, not breathing) nonetheless.

A FEW WORDS ABOUT MARKETS, THE LAW, LABOR, AND BANKS

We'll be looking shortly at examples of how executives are tapping Second Life to boost their business. In preparation for that, it would be helpful to look at a handful of the platform characteristics that will factor into their ideas.

SECOND LIFE'S THREE MARKETS: CURRENCY, REAL ESTATE, AND EQUITIES

The first of Second Life's markets concerns money.

Currency

We've been talking a lot about money changing hands in pure-play virtual businesses, but in reality all that's really changing hands is what Linden Lab defines as limited license rights, which you have in various amounts and which you can trade with others. In that respect, it's not money at all, and you can't cash in the rights you've amassed for dollars. What you can do is offer these rights for sale in a transaction denominated in dollars on an exchange that Linden Lab operates, called LindeX. One of the buyers might very well be Linden Lab. In fact, it's through its market activity that Linden Lab exercises some of its control over the market. It also maintains an automated short-circuit mechanism, not unlike the New York Stock Exchange, to cool the market during periods of unusually heavy trading. And it sets limits on how much you can buy and trade in a day.

These market matters are less important to you if you represent a business that's looking to Second Life as a marketing mechanism rather than if you're trying to make a go of it as a pure-play virtual business. As a business whose focus stays on its real-world commerce, your real costs are determined by how much developers are charging you to build your site, for example, or how much marketing consultants are charging you to help you plot your in-world marketing strategy. These services are denominated in U.S. dollars and are real-world expenses akin to working with a Web developer (which is essentially what a developer for Second Life is).

So if you're not a pure-play virtual business tycoon, exchange rate machinations and Linden Lab's role in managing its market in Lindens (monetary units) is really a side issue. That will change to the extent that the currency value of Lindens increases in conjunction with the platform's popularity. As the popularity of the platform grows, doing business denominated in Lindens will take on a whole new meaning, and interest in it won't be limited to a handful of virtual business barons. Indeed, Dutch financial institution Saxo Bank in mid-2007 was considering launching its own currency exchange. It was launching in-world banking operations to help avatars manage their Lindens, and its sights were set on getting into the currency exchange business, too, although when or if it ever will is something we'll have to wait to see.

Real Estate

There's another market in Second Life: real estate. Once Linden Lab creates a sim (technically, a single server that comes with limits on how much programming it can accommodate) and sells it to a buyer, it has expanded the market in real estate. As of mid-2007, there were about 6,000 sims under ownership, with new sims coming online at a rate of about several hundred a month, at an initial purchase cost of about $1,700 each. How much a particular sim would fetch in a subsequent resale would depend on what the owner did to improve it and where it's located.

Clearly, this market differs from real-world real estate in one fundamental way, raising a crucial question about assessing virtual land values: Second Life land is limited only by the number of servers that Linden Lab can buy and set up in its facilities in San Francisco and Dallas. Thus the market doesn't face the inconvenient limit of real-world land, which is that there's only so much of it around; once you reach that limit, you either have to start marketing land on the moon or find a way to live underwater. Nothing helps assets appreciate in value more than limited supply. Just ask the person who bought a house on the San Francisco peninsula 50 years ago. So it's important to stay tuned to see how Linden Lab handles its introduction of new sims, because in theory there's nothing to prevent it from making your land holdings worthless by flooding the market with land.

For now, though, people are making money. John Clayton, the Florida real estate agent I introduced earlier, sold a small plot of land in early 2007 for about 110,000 Lindens, or about $395 at the time, which gave him a nice, 200 percent profit, because four months earlier he had bought the land for only 35,000 Lindens. I guess you could say he flipped the property successfully. When he bought it, the land had an oceanfront view but it was hilly and not easily built upon. But, by using his own design skills, he leveled parts of it and added a waterfall, making it far more attractive to buyers.

And in one of the biggest deals to date, a transaction involving one of Second Life's most well-known properties, a Dutch media company in late March 2007 bought a group of sims known as the Amsterdam sims for approximately 13.5 million Lindens, or $50,000. It's an impressive property, replicating a downtown street scene and includes parts of Amsterdam's famed red-light district. So, for $50,000, someone is buying a set of very popular pixels on a screen. You can buy a pretty nice house in parts of the Midwest for that amount.

Equities

There's an equities market in Second Life, too, called the World Stock Exchange. It's owned by an in-world company that's in turn owned by a handful of partners, some of whose real-world names are unknown. In mid-2007, the exchange, the product of a merger between it and another exchange, called the Metaverse Stock Exchange, had some two dozen companies listed and managed a daily transaction volume of about 11 million Lindens, or about $40,000.

I mention the anonymity of some of the partners because it exposes the exchange's main problem: transparency and credibility. Would you invest U.S. dollars in shares of in-world companies, denominated in Lindens, the names of whose CEOs you may never know, and listed on an exchange whose executives you may never know?

As one of the owners of the exchange told Reuters in early 2007 coverage, "There is no protection for shareholders if the founder of a company whom everyone thought was a good investment decided to vanish." The quote is from a 24-year-old Australian named LukeConnell Vandeverre, who has disclosed his real name (it's Luke Connell), and is one of the partners in the company that owns the exchange.

As it is, the exchange itself in mid-2007 ran into its own internal problems, when a former employee allegedly used inside knowledge to steal funds. One of the results was a drop in interest by in-world companies to list on the exchange.

If the equities market today seems a little too game-like to attract major investors, tomorrow might be a different matter. The World Stock Exchange maintains a set of rules as a condition for companies being listed. If you violate the rules, you can be delisted. The exchange in mid-2007 was also musing about whether Linden Lab might play a role in punishing violators, at least the ones acting fraudulently, by wielding its leverage for violations of its terms of service, to which all residents agree as a condition of getting an avatar. But whether Linden would ever have any role to play isn't something that can really be known at this point.

At any rate, expect more rules and better transparency as that daily trading volume of $40,000 grows, because the stakes will be much higher when volume starts registering in the six and seven digits.

A NOTE ON THE LEGAL STATUS OF ANYTHING YOU CREATE IN SECOND LIFE

Although it's true that Linden Lab confers on its residents ownership rights to anything they create, exactly how protected you are in reality will not be known until virtual worlds become more commonplace and disputes over issues start receiving hearings in court.

As of mid-2007, the principal legal dispute involving Linden Lab revolves around what amounts to a side issue, what one legal analyst calls a terms of service matter, and leaves this central question of ownership unaddressed. In the one case that's gone to court, a resident allegedly managed the Second Life auction process to limit the number of bidders on a land sale, enabling him to buy an island for below what Linden was charging for an equivalent piece. (The text of the lawsuit appears in the last chapter.)

An issue more central to the ownership question arose in late 2006, when someone released a "copybot"—a program that makes unauthorized copies of objects created by Second Life residents—onto the platform, threatening residents who design clothing and objects for sale to other avatars. Because the copybot was based on Linden Lab programming, several hundred business owners closed their doors and brought a good chunk of the platform's economic activity to a halt to protest what they feared was an incursion into their rights of ownership. Linden Lab disavowed the copybot, saying it was a rogue act, and as of mid-2007 no lawsuit had been filed. But the incident reveals the fragility of what "ownership" means in a world in which everything exists in pixels.

Another case to watch, dubbed the "Sexbed Stealer" case by some, involves alleged copyright infringement. At issue is a virtual bed on which avatars, working in pairs, can have carnal fun. The bed was reportedly duplicated by an avatar without authorization of the creator and copies of it sold. The case was new as of mid-2007, so it was too early to know where it was heading.

At any rate, some legal analyses suggest that the rights—the copyright and intellectual property rights—could protect only designs, or the ideas behind the designs, and not necessarily the objects themselves. On this way of thinking, if you design a pair of jeans for avatars, the design is protected, but the individual pair of jeans isn't necessarily protected. I suppose that raises this question: If someone steals a pair of virtual jeans out of a virtual closet, is it really stealing if there are no ownership rights in the pair of jeans itself?

Whatever other cases are coming down the pike, there's no reason to suppose that copyright and intellectual property right protection is any less solid for virtual designs than for real-world designs. "Copyright laws aren't going to change," says Stevan Lieberman, the Washington patent attorney. "If you build something there, and it's worthy of copyright protection—that is, if it's not a complete steal of something else, as a lot of this stuff in Second Life is—then you have rights into it. The real problem is that people aren't filing their copyrights. And if you don't file your copyright, you don't get all the goodies that come with copyright. It's the same in Second Life. U.S. rules specifically state that you may either file your copyright prior to publication, or within three months of publication, if you want the goodies. The goodies are statutory damages, the transferring of the burden of proof to the other side, and the possibilities of attorney's fees."

But if you don't file, as Lieberman says, you get none of those protections. So until residents get serious about filing copyrights on their in-world work, their protection could be limited.

A QUICK WORD ON THE PLATFORM'S LABOR MARKET

A key consideration for you in setting up a presence in Second Life is your strategy for "staffing up" your property. It's one thing to create a terrific place at which avatars can hang out, enjoying whatever interactive features you've created; it's another to maintain a meaningful way to communicate with your visitors. Sure, you can create all sorts of ways to deliver information about your business to your guests; among other things, you can greet everyone who arrives with a note card on which you can provide an introductory message and contact information, reducing the likelihood that you'll lose these visitors should they be interested in your products or services and want an easy way to learn more. You can also maintain kiosks and other types of information delivery systems throughout your space. Really, there's no reason why visitors can't get whatever information from you that they want. What's more, you can always provide them with a link to your Web site.

However, don't assume that the availability of information is the same thing as a robust presence in Second Life. Just as people entering a store, restaurant, or office wonder about the vitality of the operation if the environment they enter is empty, avatars arriving at a location are far more apt to have a positive first impression if someone else is there. It's partly for this reason that many in-world pure-play businesses employ greeters. These are simply residents who agree to work a shift and hang out at a location to greet people and answer questions. Pay varies greatly, depending on whether the employees are just greeting people or actually making themselves available to answer questions. But typically we're not talking about very big amounts, and what's more, pay is denominated in highly depressed Linden dollars. So you might pay an avatar a hundred Linden dollars or so to spend an hour at your location. That's literally pennies, but it's enough for the avatar to make enough money to buy a pair of jeans.

Certainly many pure-play in-world businesses, particularly clubs, effectively maintain a workforce like this, with paid avatars mainly acting as greeters, dancers, and managers.

This sounds like a pretty cost-effective way to maintain a live presence at your site, but clearly that's a very risky way to go when you have crucial real-world brand equity to protect. Entrusting your brand equity to someone who in real life knows little about your business and who's earning pennies to represent you is to put more faith in people than perhaps is warranted, particularly if you don't know who the person is beyond his or her in-world identity. If nothing else, just being able to maintain some certainty that your employees will show up for work when they say they will is a major challenge.

And yet hiring a real person, at real-world wages, to maintain an avatar at your site is cost-prohibitive, at least until you build a reasonable amount of traffic to your site, and not just traffic but serious traffic— traffic consisting of visitors who are really there to tap your business and not just to look around out of curiosity.

In the end, as nice as it would be to have a live person at your site, at least during certain times of the day, you'll just have to opt for an information-only approach and hope that all the interactive attractions you have in place will be enough to represent your brand well. The fact is that this is the approach taken by most real-world brands in Second Life. What this approach has done, though, is give the serious side of Second Life—that is, the side beyond all the clubs, beaches, and malls—the look and feel that many downtowns have at night or on weekends, when all the people who work in all those office towers are in their faraway homes in the suburbs.

"Generally speaking, it's a big, empty world," says Raz Schionning, director of Web services for American Apparel, the first real-world retailer to set up shop on the platform, although the company stopped maintaining its project in mid-2007 while reassessing its viability.

Dave Levinson of Cranial Tap has been developing a cost-effective way to keep your property staffed through the use of a receptionist bot, an automated avatar that employs rudimentary artificial intelligence to greet visitors and answer basic questions on a 24/7 basis. But deploying one of these bots is probably something that will be more realistic tomorrow rather than today. "If somebody said, 'We must have this, and here are our requirements,' we'd take that request under consideration," says Levinson. "But the technology just isn't quite where we want it to be yet."

Levinson is using a bot at his Cranial Tap headquarters in Second Life. His greeter, named Tia Lisle, stands at a receptionist desk to welcome visitors and to inform them that she's a bot, not a regular avatar. She also invites the visitors to ask her questions. Levinson is probably right that the bot approach needs a bit more time to get the bugs worked out, but given the complexities of artificial intelligence—one of the holy grails of computer programming—that shouldn't come as a surprise. Here's an excerpt from a conversation I had with the bot in mid-2007. I was looking for Costal del

Sol, a Second Life resort developed by Cranial Tap and located on the same island as the company's office.

Tia Lisle: Hello. Welcome to Cranial Tap Headquarters. My name is Tia. I am the receptionist bot for Cranial Tap. To have a conversation with me please say, "Hi, Tia." I can only respond to chat, so no IMs [instant messages] please.

Me: Hi, Tia.

Tia Lisle: Greetings. To stop speaking with me, please say, "Bye, Tia." Now, what can I do for you?

Me: Where is the resort?

Tia Lisle: The resort? Where is it?

Me: Yes, do you know where it is?

Tia Lisle: This was not a yes or no question. Where it is is hard to find. I can ask someone about it.

Me: Is this where Cranial Tap is?

Tia Lisle: Yes, I think this is where Cranial Tap is, but I'm not completely sure.

Me: Are you working?

Tia Lisle: Everything is running smoothly.

Me: Are you busy today?

Tia Lisle: I am never too busy to talk with you.

Me: Have there been a lot of people here today?

Tia Lisle: No, I don't think there are any.

Me: Are there any games here?

Tia Lisle: No, I don't think there are any.

Me: Is there a chair here?

Tia Lisle: I believe there is one, yes.

Me: Are there any people here now?

Tia Lisle: Oh, no. I don't think there are any.

Me: How much does it cost to rent a room [in the resort]?

Tia Lisle: Normally I would search the Web right now, but that seems like a silly question.

As I said, the challenges of artificial intelligence are widely known, and Levinson in our conversation made it clear that in this early stage of the technology the main purpose of the bot is to welcome visitors and offer to summon a real person, and that's exactly what the bot did during our interaction. While I was having this exchange with Tia Lisle, a real avatar from Cranial Tap arrived, and asked whether he could assist me. So, when looked at from the standpoint of having someone to greet visitors without wrestling with the challenges of maintaining an employee from the in-world labor market, the receptionist bot performed admirably well, giving you an option for staffing up your business, although one that might work better in a year or two rather than today.

At any rate, bots in the future will give you more options than just using them as greeters. You will be able to use them as virtual assistants, for example, and have them offer your guests the opportunity to check their e-mail if you're holding a meeting with them. That's one function for them that Levinson has in mind. Or you can program them to be your on-site entertainment. After all, bots in a group playing "Tom Sawyer" don't need to carry on a conversation; they just need to *rock*.

More important, current weaknesses of the bot approach point to what is really your chief way to maintain a presence at your site, at least until deploying virtual staff becomes economical: inviting visitors to send you an e-mail so you can quickly deploy your avatar and get onto the platform. You might call this an alert-and-respond system, in which arriving avatars trigger an instant message to you or someone else in your company or organization who's on standby and who can then enter into an IM conversation with them.

YES, THERE ARE BANKS

The last time I counted, in mid-2007, there were about two dozen banks operating in the environment. These are privately owned, pure-play institutions, not virtual branches of real-world banks. However, some real-world banks at the time either had a presence or were thinking of launching one, including the Dutch institution, Saxo Bank, and Wells Fargo, which was operating some ATMs.

The business model of the pure-play institutions couldn't be simpler: You "pay" the bank's owner, the individual avatar, the amount in Linden dollars you want to deposit; when you want to make a withdrawal, you ask the owner to pay you back. Meanwhile, your balance accrues interest, typically something around 1 percent, although if the bank is offering to compound interest daily, it's usually something less, around 0.10 percent. The lower rate makes sense, because when interest is compounded daily the balance can grow quickly, and you can see giant annual returns, something on the order of 40 percent.

Opening an account typically takes about five seconds: You activate an ATM, and then "pay" the owner your deposit. You shouldn't be surprised if the bank doesn't even ask you to fill out a form, since it already knows who you are; information on your avatar (its name, the date it became a resident, among other things) is in the Second Life database, to which all residents have access. Taking out a loan isn't much more complicated than making a deposit.

What's hard to know, since these banks are unregulated, is what they're doing with your money. And that's an important question, since in some cases they seem to have a lot of it. Probably the most widely publicized bank is Ginko Financial, which operates several hundred ATMs and in early 2007 reportedly had collected more than half a million dollars from depositors. But the shine on the bank's star has dimmed considerably. In mid-2007 it precipitated a run on its coffers when it had trouble meeting its obligations to depositors.

The bank's problems shouldn't be taken as emblematic of the wider virtual banking industry, but they make clear the central problem of in-world commerce as it's presently constituted on the platform. Levels of transparency are at the discretion of the bank, so your money is literally in a financial black box.

Be this as it may, it's important for you to know that these virtual financial institutions are present in the environment in a big way and are poised to get bigger, at least if Ginko's problems are an aberration. If the business model you develop on the platform in any way entails avatars spending Linden dollars with you, the health of these banks as going concerns isn't a small matter, because residents are in fact holding their money in them.

At the same time, bank ATMs can be a draw to your property; avatars with money on deposit go to locations with ATMs for their bank, so working out an arrangement with a bank to locate an ATM on your property not only gives avatars a reason to go there but it also gives them a place to get their money if they decide to spend some of it with you.

A LOOK AT SOME TEST MODELS

W e're now at a point where it makes sense to look at some models of how some businesses and individuals are leveraging the unique environment of Second Life. I tried to pick models that represent a range of different types of players and approaches. This is the only practical way to explore what's possible, because there are hundreds of real-world companies operating a virtual presence and possibly thousands more individuals trying to make money in pure-play businesses. You can't look at them all, and many of them do not have much to teach you. But, once you get on the platform, you can investigate what's going on. At the back of the book, I've included what I believe is a representative list of the range of real-world companies with a virtual presence as of mid-2007.

THE ANTI-COOL APPROACH, OR HOW AN ACCOUNTING FIRM BECOMES HIP

Accounting firms are the antithesis of hip, at least to my mind, and accounting is the last business you'd expect to find on Second Life, which is why it was the first business I looked for when I went on my hunt for virtual business models. What I found was Arlene Ciroula's firm, KAWG&F, a regional player in corporate accounting with 80 accountants, about two dozen support staff members, and five offices, all of them in the southern Maryland area.

Ciroula in late 2006 was reading *Business Week* while on a flight and came across an article about Second Life and sensed immediately that there was a business application to this platform, but she wasn't quite sure how it might apply to her firm. "I just knew we were looking at something radically new that would be important years down the road and decided we had to be there in some fashion," she said.

Back at the office, she opened an account and, like millions of others, plopped onto Second Life's Orientation Island and started looking around. At the same time, she enlisted the help of her firm's IT chief, and together they put together what has possibly become the first virtual outpost for accountants.

As I mentioned earlier, H&R Block entered the space at around the same time, and in a pretty big way, too, by developing a sizable plot of land and, in fine Second Life fashion, creating a highly

interactive environment. To publicize its Tango tax preparation product, it gives away a pair of dancing shoes to visiting avatars and operates a dance floor on which avatars can use their shoes to dance the Tango. So in one fell swoop it's made all the right moves as a virtual business: leveraging the uniqueness of the environment by giving its avatars an interactive experience in a way that only a three-dimensional platform can, and linking that experience directly to its brand equity by tying the activity—Tango dancing—to its new Tango product.

But if we view H&R Block as a tax preparation service rather than as an accounting firm, then the laurel for first accounting firm in Second Life goes to KAWG&F, and what this firm is doing is far more modest—but also far more replicable. If yours is a small operation, you're not going to have the resources of H&R Block, so installing something that involves complex programming like the Tango dance floor is a gold-plated option that might not be available to you.

KAWG&F, on the other hand, has simply opened an office. It's in a modern single-tenant office building in its own sim, called

CPA Island. The office looks like anything you'd find in a Class A commercial building. The building is glass-encased, with double doors in front for entry. The floor is hardwood throughout, topped in front by a stylish rug. Art pieces and a large aquarium create a trendy edginess that sets off nicely against the sleekness of the rest of the building, almost like Starbucks meeting a Scandinavian dental lab. There's a fine-looking desk, with a vase of fresh flowers, and to one side a sitting area with a recent issue of *Harper's Bazaar*. Off to the other side is a handsome conference area in an open-space design, and down in front, a vivid red, ultramodern modular art piece with a sitting space that's large enough for several avatars to meet for tea. Parked in front is a green Solstice GXP, Pontiac's new two-seater sports car.

Everything in the decor telegraphs the message that this is a serious firm doing serious work. Indeed, the only feature that would set the office apart from something you'd find in a suburban office building is its location: it's sitting off by itself on an otherwise deserted island, giving it the feel of a building dropped by space aliens hastening to leave the planet.

What you won't find is much that's interactive. On the reception desk is a note inviting you to take a survey about your financial planning needs by clicking on a laptop that sits on the desk. Clicking on the laptop gets you transported to the company's Web site. Once you're there, you are prompted to answer up to 25 questions about how you're managing your household assets, and then you're asked if it's time to consider securing professional financial advice.

More such questionnaires will likely be coming if the company maintains its Second Life presence. Ciroula was looking into adding what she calls a decision tree, a more targeted questionnaire that would send visitors to certain departments within the company based on their accounting needs. "The IRS has called, so you need help with an audit, or you're interested in our business valuation services," she says, giving examples of how the survey

would work. "Avatars would have an opportunity to submit contact info, which would be e-mailed to the appropriate salesperson. The whole Q&A could be collapsed into an e-mail to the firm."

Ciroula has been talking with a company called Jnana, which provides the kind of Q&A software she's looking for, but she wants to wait until traffic on Second Life grows. "Our goals have been to learn how to use this platform, so we've been in observation mode for a while," she says.

Given how little the firm has invested to get to this point, taking a wait-and-see position probably makes sense.

Ciroula says it costs her about $100 a month to lease her space from the developer who built the property, plus it cost an initial $50 to acquire the furniture, which is all off-the-shelf. Originally she had used her free allocation of land—512 square meters that all new premium account holders are entitled to—for the office, but she closed that down and moved everything to this new space to exercise more control over her traffic. "We had the small piece of 'first land' and got our inventory and the office constructed, but it was on the mainland and had no zoning, so I wasn't crazy about that," she says. In this new location the office is far less likely to be a target of griefing by mischief makers, she adds.

To attract traffic, the firm advertises in the classified section of the Second Life search engine under the search terms "accounting" and "tax." When its listing comes up, you can teleport to the office or send an instant message, which goes to Ciroula's e-mail. The last time she tracked the virtual office's traffic, it was getting about half a dozen visits a day.

"We could also advertise in in-world publications (newsletters and magazines made available to avatars) for added exposure, but right now it's not worth our while," she says. "If and when in-world business gets larger, though, and the U.S. starts putting its hand in the virtual till, the model for us changes."

In other words, as the early adopter among accounting firms, Ciroula's company will be top-of-mind when in-world business-people need professional help to deal with a tax-hungry federal government that has just discovered virtual commerce.

So for now, once your avatar enters the office, your principal activity is to leave as quickly as possible to take the survey on the company's Web site. In Ciroula's view, that might be all they need at the moment. "Right now we just want to be there and have the door open," she says. "It's minimal for us right now from a cost standpoint, and we have the advantage of being an early adopter, giving us a chance to have a role in how this technology will be shaped in the future. Since we're the only accounting firm there, we get contacted for our views on things, positioning us for thought leadership in the future."

ATTORNEY BUSINESS DEVELOPMENT IN A NEW KEY

Between February 10 and late March of 2007, intellectual property rights attorney Stevan Lieberman received more than 500 e-mails originating from contacts he made at Second Life. In the 12 months prior to that, he had received something over 1,000, which means that his e-mail traffic from his virtual networking in mid-2007 was growing at a rate of about 190 percent a month. "The pace is picking up big time," he says.

So is the money. By late March 2007, after spending about a year getting familiar with Second Life and meeting other attorneys and networking with hundreds of avatars, he'd taken on two new clients and billed about $7,000 in fees. That's not a grand amount by the standards of a big-city law firm, but it's not a bad start given his small investment—$150—and the kind of work he had to do to get the business: dress up as an orange triceratops and talk to people from all walks of life. "Most of the time, I'm sitting on the couch fooling around with it, which is pure pleasure in any case," he says.

Even from that humble start he's developed a fairly deep list of contacts, including people who need legal work. "I got a patent application from a programmer I was buying software from in-world," he says. "We started talking about a variety of different things, and it ended up that she wanted to file a patent on some of her stuff that really was new and innovative."

As a self-described computer geek, Lieberman might be unusually well positioned to leverage Second Life for his business development; he came to the site as somebody already comfortable with novel computer interfaces and a geek's interest in programming issues. Indeed, he manages the computer network at his law firm. However, even he decided to leave most of the development of his in-world office to others, while he spends his time on the platform networking.

What Lieberman has set up is a floating office, under the name Greenberg & Lieberman, which is accessed from the ground by entering a gazebo with a striking black and white checkerboard tiled floor in a park-like, PG setting in an area called "Juwangswan." Inside the gazebo you click on a device that "teleports" you into the office floating above it.

Once you're in the sky, it's evident Lieberman has the interaction thing right. So that a presence is maintained while he's not there, avatars are directed to instructional primers on the issues of law in which Greenberg & Lieberman specialize: copyright, trademark, and patent. The primers are didactic in good Second Life fashion: The basics of copyright, for example, are explained through a narrative sketch that uses as its subject a community of illiterate monkeys.

Avatars also receive greetings inviting them to send an e-mail to the attorneys. He has more communication improvements in the works. "We're adding in more scripts to make it so people can communicate with us more easily," he says. "I'm working with a programmer on that right now. What I have currently is an indicator that tells me whenever someone hits my site."

When Lieberman talks about scripts, he's referring to the programming that's behind the operation of the interactive objects for visitors, like his legal primers.

Most of the e-mail he gets is generated not by strangers seeking legal advice but by attorneys and others he's met networking in-world and with whom he maintains regular contact. "I correspond almost daily with an attorney I met in there, who's now a local counsel for us in England," he says. "He had better pricing than the previous local counsel we had, and he's able to do the work just as well. If I'm able to save a little money in the process, why not have him do it?"

But as the population grows and in-world businesses become more numerous and more robust, business growth could follow, especially for an intellectual property attorney whose specialty includes writing patents for software, given the traffic of computer-savvy people there. For Lieberman, the cloak of autonomy that avatars wear is hardly an impediment to building the trust that can blossom into business relationships, a natural concern of anyone thinking about trying to build business on the platform. "There's a bunch of people that I started out talking to that said, 'Oh, I'll never tell anybody about me in the real world,'" he says. "And yet over time, as we've become friends, I e-mail back and forth with them regularly. One guy's an Australian, another person's from Seattle, another comes from Italy. . . ."

It is not necessary to assume that avatars' names, even though they're fictitious, are cloaking their owner's true identity. After all, the first part of the name of Lieberman's avatar, Navets Potato, is simply Stevan in reverse.

TAMING THE WILD WEST IN REAL ESTATE

Given the explosion of real estate listings on the Internet, with sites like Realtor.com and Trulia.com giving consumers increasing amounts of control over their home searches, you would expect the blue-chip real estate company Coldwell Banker to have made real-world search a part of its world when it opened its Second Life doors in late March 2007. It didn't. It launched with an in-world-only sales approach. But after several months of experiment, it did indeed branch out into real-world sales. By the third quarter of 2007 it was offering real people the option of obtaining an avatar and walking through a virtual reproduction of a real house.

As this book went to print, the company had just listed its first real-world property that it was showing virtually, a $3.1 million house for sale on Mercer Island, Washington, but Charlie Young, the company's senior vice president of marketing, sees this as an area of future growth. "Not only does this open up a whole new way of marketing a home, but it also exposes Coldwell Banker to an entirely new pool of potential customers who embrace technology and collaboration," he says.

Given the walls separating Second Life from the World Wide Web, equipping people who aren't already on the virtual platform with an avatar and getting them to the listing isn't a straightforward operation. How, and how well, Coldwell Banker can smooth this transition in the months and years ahead will be critical in determining how widespread in-world virtual house tours will become.

For this first listing, visitors to the site of the Mercer Island home's listing agent, Suzanne Lane of Coldwell Banker Bain, were given the option of viewing conventional photos of the house on Lane's Web page. They're also given the option of walking through a virtual reproduction of the house on Second Life. Visitors who wanted to exercise that option were directed to click on a link to the new accounts page on the Second Life Web site. Here they could open up a free Second Life account, just like I did when I first entered the platform. Once they opened their account, they were deposited onto Orientation Island, just as I was. From there, they could plug in the exact location of the Mercer Island house using the SLURL (the Second Life URL I talked about earlier), which was posted on Lane's Web page, and teleport directly to the listing, located on Coldwell Banker's in-world island. Then, using their navigation tools, they could walk around the house and through its rooms.

Here's the exact wording of the directions I took from Lane's Web page:

> "To tour a 3-D replica of this house in the popular virtual world Second Life, follow these steps: 1. Go to www.second life.com. 2. Register and download the free software. 3. Once

in Second Life, click on the 'Map' button in the lower right corner, and search for 'Ranchero,' which is the name of the section where the listing resides. The property inside Second Life is at the following link: http://slurl.com/secondlife/Ranchero/43/147/67." [This is a Second Life URL. It will take you to the property.]

Thus, home shoppers with no experience with Second Life could bypass everything else on the platform and go directly to Coldwell Banker's listing, making it unnecessary for them to familiarize themselves with much of the intricacies of navigating from one location to another. That's a tremendously important advantage, because it removes one of the biggest hurdles businesses face in opening up what they're doing virtually to as wide a mainstream audience as possible.

Even so, visitors still must take the time to become familiar enough with the platform's movement and camera controls to be able to move their avatar around and through the house. But David Marine, senior manager of e-marketing at Coldwell Banker, told me that navigation issues haven't appeared to be a problem.

"It's true getting to the virtual house wasn't like clicking on a link and, 'boom,' you're there, but actually we've had zero negative feedback," he says. "In fact, the listing agent gave a walk through to a guy who was in Italy, who became interested in the house. My initial reaction is that many of the people were already in Second Life, which already has more than 8 million accounts, so you already have a decent-sized user base. But I think there are other people who, because of this listing, are getting into it and checking it out."

Another company spokesperson, Michael Fischer of Gunslinger Media Relations, which handles media inquiries for Coldwell Banker, told me none of the media calls he took after announcement of the virtual tour involved in-world navigation troubles. Rather, all the calls had to do with technical glitches in getting onto the platform, probably because the visitors lacked the right graphics card on their computer or had an internal firewall that needed to be modified to allow access.

"I think the people that needed to be walked through it were really just having tech issues with their own computers or the firewalls," Fischer told me. "I really don't think Second Life posed a barrier to anyone looking to buy a home."

Coldwell Banker's location in Second Life is on a big plot of land called the "Ranchero." Prior to making the Mercer Island home available for real-world home shoppers, the company concentrated mainly on becoming a pure-play virtual real estate brokerage company for avatars already in-world. And today it continues to make that a chief focus of its Second Life experiment, although ultimately its strategy will certainly take it increasingly toward more real-world applications.

Virtual brokerage, though, makes good sense as an initial strategy for the company. Buying and selling real estate is far and away the platform's biggest pure-play commercial activity. And it makes sense for a major player like Coldwell Banker to bring to the Wild West of Second Life the kind of brokerage stability that we take for granted in the real world. That, at least, is how the company is looking at its experiment.

"We think we can bring a lot of order to the in-world transaction process," says Young.

And order is needed, Young believes. In Second Life a handful of pure-play virtual landowners are playing an outsized role in the real estate market by bundling large tracts of land together and selling them as a package, making it necessary for buyers looking for something more than a small plot to buy more than they need. "Generally speaking, land barons are selling multiple tracts of land at once rather than letting you buy one tract," says Young. "The average price for one of those tracts is $60. What we're providing is a plot of land, a home, and some furniture as a closing gift, all for about $20. So, we think we can bring price stability."

What's more, the company thinks it can help ramp up values in the same way as in real life, by creating communities in which people want to live. That means offering buyers assurance that a bar or a bail bondsman won't move in next door. "When people buy into our community, they're bound by the architecture and style and can't change that," says Young. "There are security measures. If anything happens, we're on it. We know what's happening in any of our neighborhoods at any point in time. There can't be any businesses, advertising on lawns, or signage. These are just sleepy little neighborhoods." Rental units are available in the communities, too.

The units differ, but generally what you get for your $20 is a two-room house with a patio. In "Elboya," where Coldwell Banker is selling a community with a southwestern theme, your house has hardwood floors, textured interior walls, finely detailed windows, and a tiled patio, just right for a barbecue. It's a neighborhood in which anyone would be pleased to raise their children.

The company is selling its all-virtual homes in four different communities, each taking its own stylistic path. In addition to the southwest in "Elboya," the themes are Victorian, Greek island, and traditional, which reflects what you'd see in the suburbs of Cleveland. By the end of its first day of open doors in Second Life, it had closed three sales and had 20 appointments waiting for its agents.

Some 1,500 avatars in all had visited over the first two weeks of the company's grand opening, each avatar spending about 10 minutes at the site.

As in the real world, the company's agents—four are on staff at any one time during the week, 8 a.m. to 8 p.m.—are there to walk customers through the units and speak knowledgeably about the transaction process and obtaining finance. And they can point avatars to places where they can go in-world to get their credit checked. That's a necessity, given that few avatars will have the Lindens necessary to get into their dream home without taking out a loan. After all, at $20 a home, or 5,400 Lindens, you're talking a lot of money. And there's no shortage of virtual lenders, so credit checks are needed.

"Using what we're calling our v-commerce sales tool, a virtual agent will be able to pull out a virtual notebook computer, have the prospective customer avatar touch a virtual 'palm-scanner,' and automatically go to our databases for a check against a 'no-biz' list—a database of avatars who don't keep current on their in-world debt obligations," says Jennifer Butler, a spokesperson for the company. The palm scanner also checks "past customer activity, and qualification status, and sends the response back to the virtual notebook for visual display of qualification status," she says.

As in the real world, the agents earn a fee for managing the sale, although so far these aren't real-world agents plying their trade in their off hours virtually; rather, they're avatars employed and managed by the developer the company retained to build its site. "These are real people behind the avatars," says Charlie Young.

Since the company isn't focusing on brokering existing homes, the way it does in the real world, for all practical purposes it is acting more as a developer than a broker, because the units it is selling are from its own development. Of course, avatars who buy the units are free to resell them, just as they are in real life, and it's the company's hope that the sellers will look to the company to help find buyers and make the deals happen when they're ready to put their home on the market. "We hope they'll come to us, but they don't have to," says Young.

As for profit, it's really not built into the business model, at least yet. Even proceeds from the sale of the units go back into more land purchases, so the company can sell more houses. Instead, the business is all about long-term customer building, especially with a particular demographic—computer savvy thirty-somethings—that today are fueling real-world sites like Realtor.com and Trulia.com, and are only just beginning to understand where gathering information online is best stopped and working with a real estate agent is best begun.

"This play is not about making money," says Young. "This is about making a positive impact on a new breed of consumer as it relates to our brand. If this process is a good testing ground for us, that would be a good thing for us; it would give us a channel for generating traffic to Coldwell Banker.com, and it signals our commitment to innovation."

Looking ahead, the company is intrigued by the idea of hosting get-togethers with its real-world clients and customers in 3-D offices. While this is something it will keep its eyes on, it remains in the pure conjecture stage. "What we know is that a new breed of consumer is participating in Second Life, and we want to be there and experiment as this new form of communicating is developing," says Young. "That way we're able to evolve with it and be a logical answer for consumers when they're ready for their real-word purchases. Rather than being on a two-dimensional Web site, on-line experiences in the future could be through a 3-D experience in which you're actually entering a Coldwell Banker virtual office in the real world. That's a 'could-be.'"

Getting it perceived as an innovator by tech-savvy young people isn't a small thing for the company, which in 2006 celebrated its 100-year anniversary and by its own characterization is positioning itself as both a rock-solid pillar of the country and a forward-thinking services and technology company. It can certainly claim to have all the right technology at its Ranchero site. When you teleport onto its land, the first thing you see is its giant outdoor theater, a multimedia platform in which it plans to host real-time training sessions and meetings for brokers and company owners from the 45 or so countries it's in.

In its headquarters building next to the theater, the company's hosting an interactive museum exhibit that showcases landmark moments in American history that, not coincidentally, track great

moments in the company's 100-year evolution. The exhibit pushes all the right Second Life buttons, too, because it's visually arresting and interactive at the same time, even a little educational. But it's also just a very clever way to walk the line the company wants to walk between being a solid, well-grounded company and a forward-looking company as well.

That's good corporate public relations, and there's scarcely any money to be made there, but the company hasn't entirely given up on the chance to convert a few avatars to real-world customers. Outside the exhibit you can get directed to the company's home-search site on the Web and also get linked up directly with an agent. The Ranchero opened in late March 2007. Give it time, and you can bet the company's agents will start receiving instant messages from strangely named avatars in Second Life inquiring about a home—a real-world home—they'd like to see.

THEY "SAW IT IN SECOND LIFE": THE REAL ESTATE BRIDGE FROM IN-WORLD TO YOUR WORLD

In another real estate move, John Clayton, a one-time real estate agent in Florida, was leveraging the platform in an attempt to drive Second Life's thirty-something early adopters to a real-world community that he thought was well fitted to their tastes: the San Ruffino townhouses in Dunedin, Florida.

The first 26 units of the planned development are scheduled to come online in fall 2007, and interest had been fueled at least in part by the traffic of avatars who had been entering the developer's Web site from Clayton's Second Life real estate office. Clayton has since moved into other, non-real-estate-related ventures.

The units, although at the time fairly pricey (top-end units in early 2007 were on the market for more than $1 million), were very much geared to the young-skewing population that's heavily represented on the platform. They were just the kind of condo that successful, young people would find attractive. They were large, with high-end amenities like hardwood floors, granite countertops, a covered patio, an open lanai, and private elevators. And they were low maintenance, with no yards to care for. "We actually had someone from Virginia who saw it in Second Life fly down to Florida to visit the project," says Clayton.

For Clayton, then a sales associate with Charles Rutenberg Realty in Clearwater, Florida, the San Ruffino project gave him the perfect opportunity to test the viability of Second Life as a bridge to real-world real estate. When I spoke to him in 2007, he thought the traffic he was generating, just through a few classified ads in the Second Life search engine, supported his hunch that the platform is uniquely well suited to marketing real estate in-world. "Early on I was getting a lot of hits a day," he says.

Once he knew he could attract avatars to his office, in an area called Techno City, he set out to beef up his offerings. At the time, you could go directly from his office there to a real-world real estate search site and to the site of a mortgage broker, as well as to the San Ruffino Web site. It was a path to customers that Clayton, who tapped his background in computer graphics to undertake his own 3-D development for his office, wanted to help more real estate agents follow by offering them his services. "An agent can get in for a couple of hundred dollars," he says. "For $500 they could probably get an entire office. That's a modest amount for getting a presence on a platform that's growing at a rate of 15 or 20 percent a month."

Talk about agents setting up an office is a start. But the real aim of any real estate agent would no doubt be the same as what Clayton is ultimately striving for: leveraging the 3-D environment in a way that's uniquely well suited to real estate by hosting avatars in virtual tours of properties. That's much like what Coldwell Banker has started doing.

. . .

It's also what Starwood was doing with its new aloft line of hotels. In October 2006 it opened up a virtual model. The company says its model attracted a gaggle of visitors during a demonstration period, thanks in part to a slew of high-profile events thrown at its site, including an appearance by Ben Folds, probably best known for his 1998 single "Brick."

Starwood's goal was to build buzz for its new line of moderately priced, loft-styled hotels. But it also wanted to get feedback on design and layout from potential customers after they had a chance to walk their avatars through it.

I didn't interview Starwood for this book, but according to coverage in *BusinessWeek*, the company observed how the avatars moved through the space, what areas and types of furniture they gravitated toward, and what they ignored. The company also hosted a blog for visitors to share their ideas for design tweaks after their avatar had checked out the model. In mid-2007, Clayton was working to do something similar for the San Ruffino, although he wasn't sure he'd finish it—at least not before all the units were sold. But whether he completes that build or not, it was only his first attempt at what he hopes will become a staple of virtual platforms in the future. "What could be more natural than introducing a project virtually and having hundreds of people tour it through their avatars?" he says. Like what Starwood is doing, "You could get feedback and incorporate that into your ultimate design, so when your project comes online in the real world, it's already been honed to customers' tastes."

NOT YOUR TEENAGER'S WEB: LEVERAGING THE PLATFORM TO CREATE PURE ESCAPISM

Although each example we've looked at thus far uses Second Life in a way that capitalizes on what's unique about the platform—the accounting firm maintains that conference room, for example, where an accountant could meet clients as an alternative to a conference call—we haven't seen anything that isn't an alternative to something that's already available on the Web.

The closest application we've seen so far that leverages the uniqueness of a social 3-D environment is the Coldwell Banker virtual tours, in which an avatar clicks on a model house to get teleported to the house for an actual walk-through. That's not something that's really replicable in any other medium, although really what the tour comes down to is a fancy version of the virtual tours already available on real estate companies' Web sites and on Realtor.com. The difference is that current online virtual tours are like watching little videos, with the camera scanning each room, while the Second Life tour is a 3-D walk-through that you direct yourself through your avatar. Home tours over your video iPod that some real estate brokerages make available are the closest thing to the Second Life tours, but in this case you're not the one directing what you see; the person holding the video recorder is.

What Storm Williams of MojoZoo is doing for one of his clients breaks this mold. When I talked with him in mid-2007, he was building an island that would replicate a World War II United Service Organization (USO) facility to enable deployed soldiers to interact in real time with their families. His client, Books for Soldiers, is a charity whose mission is to boost morale of deployed military personnel by making available to them free books, DVDs, CDs, or just some kind of care package that soldiers can order online and which is delivered to them through the mail by one of the organization's volunteers.

To my mind, the 3-D USO facility isn't a substitute for anything that is already available on the Web but leverages what's genuinely unique about a social 3-D environment. The closest thing to it today is instant messaging, but clearly interaction among avatars in a 3-D environment is so much more than an exchange of short text e-mails.

"If a soldier is sitting on a carrier, or they're in Kuwait or in Baghdad, they can log onto Second Life, meet their spouse in this

World War II USO dance hall, or go to the restaurant, have dinner, go dancing, or go down to the beach with the kids and play football," Williams says. "Now, it's still not like being there, but the marketing tests that we did were amazing. It's not exactly family time, but when things are blowing up around you, it's much better than instant messenging. It's really escapist, and it really improves morale."

Having this kind of morale booster available could be especially important should deployments get longer and more frequent. "There are all sorts of relationship issues with the people who stay behind when soldiers deploy," Williams says. "The deployed military has a very high divorce rate. Even with things like instant messenging and e-mail, it's still not like being at home."

For its marketing tests, Williams had soldiers log on to a specially prepared site and answer questions that he had posted. He also had conversations about the platform with testers.

In another project he's building, for a global executive placement firm, the virtual facility is intended to take pressure off clients' travel budgets without sacrificing in-depth interviews for gauging applicants' fitness for relocation by providing a place where the three parties involved—the hiring company, the placement company, and the applicant—can meet in real time. "The hiring company's location is never in the same town as the applicant, and typically the placement company is in a different location entirely, as well," says Williams. "These are high-end jobs, and the placement company does a lot of prep work of the candidate to make sure they understand the job. A lot of weeding out needs to happen to make sure the applicant is the right person for the right job. That's how they built their reputation."

In the works is an in-world interview studio, where the placement firm can interview the candidate and help in the weeding-out process, "because you can't send a person from Milan to China on a lark for an interview," he says. Conversations will be able to take place outside the studio as well. He's combining the 3-D technology of Second Life with Skype, the Internet phone system. "So you can have you avatar running around in Second Life with a Skype pager stuck to it, and anybody else using Skype you can talk to," says Williams. "You don't have to type out the page. You can actually hear them."

As most developers do when building a location in Second Life, Williams and his team are building their sites using a combination of existing and custom-designed elements—objects, textures, and programming—in a process that any art director would be familiar with. "It's the same thing as doing a print ad for a magazine," he says. "Sometimes you have the opportunity to use stock photography, and sometimes you have to go out and shoot it yourself."

Williams is building the USO and global placement facilities each on its own island. Having ample space for the projects is part of the reason, but more important to Williams is the control of having an entire island, since each island is built on its own server. "Nobody can move in next door and put in a strip club," he says. "No one can come in and put in an application that's going to eat up all your processing power and slow down any simulations you have on it."

These aren't minor considerations, given the importance of having good experiences to offer visiting avatars. "If you want to put your brand out there, you want to make sure it's a good brand experience," Williams says. "So we always pitch an island (to our clients), and then if they get an island, we always tell them, 'Well, you might as well use this space.'"

What that gives you is ample space for a facility that lets you leverage the 3-D and social aspects of the platform to their maximum effect.

SOCIAL INTERNET 3.0 IN 3-D SPACE

Taking the idea of the social Internet one step further than virtual meet-ups is a rating company, RatePoint, that in early 2007 extended its service to Second Life by enlisting avatars to go around the platform as critics, saying what they like and don't like about their fellow avatars.

In the real world, RatePoint manages a tool for consumers to rate Web sites, and the company then groups these consumer raters together based on the what and how of the sites they rate, creating in effect groups of like-minded people who can be networked together so they can leverage their commonalities to their benefit.

The premise goes like this: All the people who love Microsoft's site, MSN.com, for example, were they to know about each other, would benefit from knowing about other sites that their fellow Microsoft site lovers like. Conversely, people who don't like the Microsoft site can learn what sites other Microsoft site haters like, or they can come together for other purposes, given that they start with this common bond. It's classic social media stuff.

"We're able to group you up with people who rated the same Web site and project the type of Web sites you might like or have a social interaction with," says Chris Bailey, CEO of RatePoint, which is based in Boston. "Microsoft is a good example, because it tends to polarize people," he says. "You have people who love Microsoft and people who hate it, so you can create groups of like-minded people. Microsoft for you might be a five, for me it might be a one, and we also have comments that go along with them. These comments are displayed in a prioritized order based on your group of like-minded people. The comments most important to you flow to the top of the list."

RatePoint now has brought this service to Second Life. In March 2007 it opened a café with a large deck overlooking a beach and, at least in its early months, was offering regular concerts, typically on weekends, as a vehicle for generating traffic to its site. The concerts are live video streams of real-world bands that avatars can watch while seated in the café or on the deck. There's dancing, too. And if you don't want to watch the band, you can go to the beach, where among other things you can go hang gliding.

The live concerts and other activities play well in the Second Life environment because they meet that critical test that any good virtual presence must have: something for avatars to do. At the same time, the events give the company something to advertise each week in the special events section of the in-world search site. The result has been to make the RatePoint Cafe a relatively busy traffic destination out of the gate. "It's getting a lot of traction," Bailey says.

More important from the company's standpoint, its high-interactivity presence generated enough interest in its rating program early on so that within just a few weeks of its launch it had recruited what Bailey estimates is several thousand avatars to sign up as raters, and now there's this army of avatars going around rating other avatars on a scale of one to five, whether those other avatars want to be rated or not. If an avatar knows where all the good concerts are in Second Life, for example, and that's important to you, you might rate that avatar highly, and also note the avatar's concert knowledge specifically in your comments. Now, other avatars that do ratings have that information, giving them an avatar they can contact to learn about upcoming concerts.

In a sense, what the in-world rating service does is fill the credibility gap that exists on the platform today, since avatars are represented by assumed names, leaving you only their appearance and your own sense of their trustworthiness based on your conversations with them by which to judge them. Now you have this other handle to grab onto: the views of others who have rated the avatar.

As it is, Linden Lab built a rating system into its program that at one time was available for anyone to use as part of the controls. The rating system has since been removed, but even when it was in place, it was pretty limited. It only looked at whether you liked the way the avatar looked or whether you were impressed with the objects the avatar had built. The rating system never let you go into sticky value-type judgments, nor did it let you post specific comments. Also, the Linden system allowed for just a positive rating. The RatePoint system doesn't have that limitation. It enables you to indicate negative views by its one-to-five scale.

The company has thus integrated its real-world business into Second Life in a rather clever way, providing residents with a tool that goes some way to closing a very real gap in their ability to assess other avatars effectively. This isn't unimportant to you if you're thinking about integrating your own business into Second Life because you'll want to have some handle on the credibility of avatars you're thinking about working with. You might recall that Ciroula, the accounting firm COO, used as a crude proxy for assessing the credibility of other avatars whether or not they had a paid account. If they did, then Ciroula at least knew that the people behind the avatars had made some investment in their in-world personae; if they didn't, Ciroula understood that they could be what might be called a *dead-ender*, someone who stands to lose nothing by acting without accountability.

As a side note, it's not unusual to meet, and conduct business with, other people solely through their avatars, in some cases never learning their real names. Indeed, you're going to meet an executive who launched his company's in-world presence with the help of a 3-D builder he met in Second Life and with whom he conducted business entirely in an avatar-to-avatar transaction. Others I interviewed for this book did the same thing. In some cases, they later came to know their contact's real–world identity, but in other cases, the transaction remained entirely at the avatar level. Although

RatePoint's system is far from foolproof, it would be hard for an avatar to dismiss or credibly disavow negative ratings from a range of different avatars. So now you've got a pretty good indicator that this is an avatar with whom you would want to do business only with your eyes wide open.

The company's long-term goal is to grow its ranks of in-world raters because then these avatars could be harvested to provide ratings on the real-world side of its business, which Bailey says will expand beyond Web sites in the second half of 2007 to include products. So the company has already reaped some rewards from its foray into Second Life because its potential pool of real-world raters had expanded by several thousands in just a few weeks, and all it had to do to spur this growth was create a virtual hangout spot and offer a free coffee mug to avatars who can only pretend to drink coffee.

GIVING UNIVERSAL DESIGN
A WHOLE NEW MEANING

If you follow real estate trends to any degree, you've probably heard of the universal design movement. It's an effort to change the way the professionals who design and build houses and commercial buildings and the way people who live and work in these places think about accessibility, not just for the disabled but for the frail and anyone with temporary special needs, like a pregnant woman or a teenager with a broken leg. The idea is that residential and commercial properties that follow certain design principles can be made to accommodate anyone while remaining comfortable and attractive for people for whom accessibility features aren't necessary. In homes, for example, what we're talking about are simply features like front doors without thresholds, lower kitchen cabinets, levers instead of door knobs, and walk-in showers.

John Paul, the CEO of a for-profit company that helps nonprofits juice up their performance, thinks that no environment is better

than a virtual one for bringing down barriers to accessibility by making all physical barriers a thing of the past. His company, AssociationWorks, based in Dallas, launched its Second Life presence in February 2007 in part to create a total barrier-free meeting space for its clients, including the National Multiple Sclerosis Society.

"Individuals who have multiple sclerosis can meet and, in a sense, not have any disabilities in that platform," says Paul. "They'll be able to sit at a table, talk about things, and share their experiences in a relatively safe way. Especially for people with mobility issues, this would be a chance for them to shed those problems, for a moment in time at least, and interact in a different way, which might be beneficial to them at lots of different levels."

If you count distraction as a barrier, virtual meetings can bring down that one, too. "What's happening in a lot of meetings, like a brainstorming session, involving people who know each other on a classic conference call, is that little gets done," he says. "The calls get routine and pretty dull. People are multitasking usually, rather than actually focusing. It would be much tougher for them to multitask if they also have to interact with their colleagues in Second Life, so it's an issue of being more focused."

When I spoke with Paul in mid-2007, he was gearing up to host his first meeting and was still ironing out specifics, including the

Internet phone service he would use so that meeting attendees could communicate orally rather than by text via instant messaging, but to Paul there was little doubt that businesses and nonprofits would be demanding this kind of virtual meeting service in the future once they get their first taste of it.

"Nonprofits are always looking for ways to save money, especially on travel, and this would be a way for them to meet and interact and probably get 70 percent of the social benefit of being together," he says.

To be sure, he believes that much of the reason he expects people meeting virtually by avatar to be engaged is the novelty of the whole thing, but the effectiveness of virtual meetings will carry beyond that and become the forum of choice for certain types of meetings.

"What I'm hoping is, we can get past the 'wow' factor and see this is as a good way of doing things," he says.

Paul intimated that he gets a return on his investment in the platform if his clients start using his virtual meeting space regularly or create their own space as part of the facility he's built, because in using the space they're affirming that his company has introduced them to a value-added service, and that translates into satisfied clients and better client retention.

As it is, his company spent next to nothing—only a few hundred dollars—to build and maintain its virtual space.

One of his colleagues met the 3-D builder they employed in Second Life, an avatar named Kathy Carlton, and hooked her up with Paul in a virtual meeting. "Like in a typical meeting with an architect, we talked about the look and feel of what we wanted," says Paul. "We wanted it to be professional-looking, with lots of open space and office space, a meeting room where people could look at PowerPoint presentations and videos, and with meeting tables. She came back with ideas, and it was all done online. I've never actually talked to her."

The builder would show Paul what she had in stock, from previous projects, and then tweak the objects—whether a room or a piece of furniture like a desk—based on their conversations. The development process took about 10 days from start to finish.

"I would be standing next to her, and she would open up a box and the room or the piece of furniture would appear," says Paul. "So I could actually look at it and walk through it."

Carlton also helped Paul find the land on which the office is located, and she guided him through the leasing process. After finishing the office, she landscaped the exterior, creating a park-like setting that includes a duck pond and, in a pastoral touch, a spot where you can feed birds.

For Paul, the ducks and the birds are symbolic of the kind of enhanced environment you can create in-world, which is why he thinks nonprofits that leverage his new facility are really leveraging the uniqueness of the virtual platform—a platform in which physical barriers become a thing of the past.

WITH PROMO BLAST, MARKETING FLOODGATES OPEN

If there's any one point in Second Life's short history that marks its turn from a gamer's haven to a commercial marketers' mecca, it's when Los Angeles–based clothing company American Apparel entered the platform with a splashy party in June 2006. Prior to the company's entry, Second Life was entirely the domain of its residents, with every commercial enterprise a pure-play virtual business. The only exceptions were a few temporary forays by entertainment companies—Warner Bros. and Twentieth Century Fox, among them—that hosted some splashy promotion events.

And that's what you'd expect: In operation for only a couple of years and with a population of only about 120,000 residents—at a time when a virtual game like World of Warcraft was boasting something on the order of 7 million players—the platform just wasn't on the radar screen of corporate executives.

It wasn't on American Apparel's radar screen either, even though the company's director of Web services, Raz Schionning, had been a resident since 2005, when he had read an article about it in *Scientific American*. Schionning's "aha!" moment came in early 2006 during a conversation with a marketing consultant, Wes Keltner, CEO of The Ad Option, in Lexington, Kentucky. Schionning and Keltner were talking about opportunities for leveraging the popularity of games like World of Warcraft by marketing American Apparel on those platforms in some way, and it was Keltner who introduced the idea of looking into Second Life. "I said, 'That is just brilliant. That's a fantastic idea,'" reports Schionning.

The absence of other retailers particularly caught Schionning's eye; it gave American Apparel the rare opportunity to break marketing ground as the first real-world company to enter the space. That was appealing even if in the end the effort produced more buzz than business boost. "We had no expectation of what it might result in," Schionning says.

What the company did know, though, was that the demographics were right for the company's line of socially conscious, urban youth "hipster" clothes: "Second Life residents were in the right age range; they were fairly balanced by gender; and we could infer certain things about their economic status by the fact that they needed a high-speed Internet connection and a pretty powerful computer to be on there. So, the chance to interact with a couple hundred thousand of these people made sense to us. We said, 'Let's see what happens if we reach out to them. Who knows what it might bring?'"

Working with Keltner, Schionning contracted with a well-regarded in-world developer, Aimee Weber, to build the company's virtual space. Schionning sent Weber photos and layouts of American Apparel stores, arranged conference calls with her and with architects who worked on American Apparel stores and also its store merchandisers. He also had avatar-to-avatar meetings with her on the platform. "In many ways it was like we were building a true retail space," he says.

Weber produced for them an all-glass, two-story building on a beachfront with lots of exterior event space. Inside were racks of colorful T-shirts and pants, copies of the company's trademark casual wear, and, on the walls were oversized black-and-white art prints.

To give its site a splashy launch, the company hosted two events—a preopening party for invited guests in May followed by the grand opening a month later—and attracted hundreds of avatars and generated for the company a wave of media coverage that it rode until it put its site on hold, in mid-2007. "We had no idea anyone would take notice," says Schionning.

The events weren't without hitches. Faced with the issue of Second Life's limited grid capacity, the company had to manage the flow of avatars to its parties carefully, something that it would be better equipped to handle today because of what's been learned in the year since about maximizing grid capacity (for example, holding an event at the corner of four islands to leverage server capacity). "On an island you can only have about 50 people at one time, so we pretty much hit the maximum within three minutes of starting the event," says Schionning, "and then we just had a queue; anybody who tried to get in just had to wait their turn."

On the negative side, the launch generated a little backlash from some of the platform's early adopters, who used the event as a way to express their grievances with the way Second Life was evolving. The group, calling itself the "Second Life Liberation Army," ran around the event wielding weapons and making political statements that were not specifically directed at the company but rather at the lack of a formal process for residents to take collective action and set governing policies. As one of the mischief makers said of the group's decision to attack American Apparel, "It's because of its [the company's] representative value."

"I certainly understand that sentiment," says Schionning. "We kind of broke into this world in their eyes."

But that was then. As of mid-2007 there were possibly hundreds of real-world companies represented on the platform, and the number is growing weekly, signaling unmistakably the direction in which the platform is headed, for better or for worse. And while some disruptive incidents continue as a part of the environment's culture, they're almost entirely driven by pranksters, not protesters, and they attract little support beyond the ranks of the pranksters themselves.

StormWilliams of the marketing consulting firm MojoZoo likens what happened to what America Online (AOL) experienced when it first opened its platform to advertisers. That move offended some early adopters of AOL. But in the drive to leverage all the opportunities of the platform, the critics were outnumbered.

"Naysayers in the very beginning [of something like this] are typically very loud, but they're squelched by the sheer thundering herds coming over the top of them," says Williams. "In Second Life, there's a very hard-core, long-term community, but I've yet to meet any of them. I might some day, but I think the sheer thundering herd of people coming onto the platform is bringing a very different idea of what they want it to be."

Of course, acceptance by the community and getting traffic from that community to your site are two different things, and while American Apparel rode out the acceptance issue, it continued to struggle with the traffic problem up until it put its site on hold. After enjoying daily traffic in the hundreds while it basked in the lingering glow of its launch parties, the company in early 2007 watched traffic to its site ebb because not enough interactivity was built into it. Unless you wanted to pick up some clothes for your avatar or take a side trip to the company's Web site, there was little for an avatar to do there.

Schionning was well aware of those limitations, and that's certainly something he's looking at. "If you really want to make people come back to you, it's similar to your commitment to building a Web site: You can't just build a site and expect people to come. You have to make a reason for them to come and a reason for them to come back, and a reason for them to spend time there," he says.

As a result, the company has been rethinking its approach to the site with the aim of taking it to a different level, one with the kind of interactivity that will give avatars a reason to return and spend some time there. Some ideas under discussion: hosting fashion shows and letting avatars design their own clothes. But both of these come with hurdles, says Schionning. The fashion show is premature until in-world visual resolution improves enough to enable sharp reproduction of clothing details, like stitching, otherwise the details that set one brand part from another are missed; and self-designed clothing is problematic from the standpoint of the company's retailing approach, which isn't based on consumers deciding what the company's clothes should look like. "That's not what we do," says Schionning. "Our stores aren't about designing your own clothes."

Schionning has also entertained the idea of offering products exclusive to Second Life, but that also raises issues about how that fits into the company's retailing approach. "On some levels exclusive products make sense, because we would be creating something that connects with the environment, but that's also not what we do," he says. "And would that somehow create confusion about who we are and what we represent?"

Companies that have had the benefit of observing the experiences of the early adopters have developed in-world properties that clearly reflect the evolution in best practices. Many of the sites of the car companies, like the Scion site for Toyota and the Pontiac site for GM, offer avatars plenty to do: taking a car for a test drive, for starters, And H&R Block's "Tango" dance floor hits the right notes on interactivity, as does Coldwell Banker's Ranchero site, among many others. More of that has to happen before companies like American Apparel can start to reap the full benefits of the Second Life community, Schionning believes. "There are certainly some bright examples out there, some who are getting it right," he says.

Given what it's invested, the company believes that it got things right just by virtue of being there first. Schionning wouldn't say what he paid Weber to develop the company's site, but the cost was low—"less than a typical ad banner campaign," he says—and that if it got nothing out of the site beyond the 10,000 pieces of virtual clothes it sold over its year and a half in-world for a few hundred Linden dollars apiece (about $10,000 total) and some marketing buzz, it was well worth it. "At the end of the day, it worked as a branding vehicle," he says. "If they came to our space and they poked around a little bit, we made some kind of impression on them, and the next time they see a banner ad or they see a print ad, well, then, it all helps in the grand scheme of things."

The bottom line for him: "We've learned something. And now the big question is, 'What do we do next?'"

THE **STARTING POINT** FOR YOU

Based on the lessons learned from the selection of early adopters we've looked at, you can formulate your approach into Second Life into a series of steps for leveraging this three-dimensional social Internet environment. They can be summarized into six points.

1. Determine What about Your Product or Service Lends Itself Best to a 3-D, Social Media Environment

It is crucial that you determine what it is about your product or service that works best in a 3-D social environment because viewing the platform as an extension of your Web site sends the wrong message to residents. You're telling them that you don't get it. Not getting it is probably okay for the early adopters, because, really, who did fully get it? But the models are there now, and you can't ignore them.

If your business involves a consumer product, you have a pretty straightforward challenge for capitalizing on what Second Life does best: let avatars use your product in-world. It's relatively easy to let avatars ride around on your motorcycle if that's what you sell.

If yours is a business-to-business product, like a hydraulic valve, your job is harder in some ways, but in other ways it's not. It makes little sense to invest the time, energy, and money into devising something that demonstrates the qualities of your valve to an audience of avatars; what does make sense, though, is to use the collaborative strength of the platform to host in-world meetings of people who care about your valves: the people who design them, the people who sell them, and the people who buy them. In these cases, your model is what AssociationWorks is doing: providing virtual meeting space that improves upon the classic conference call by heightening participants' interest in what's being discussed.

If yours is a consumer service, like homeowner's insurance, you want to let people choose from options and purchase their policy right there, just as they would in a bricks-and-mortar office. That might seem pretty boring, but nothing's stopping you from hosting a café with a band or other entertainment at your office, just as RatePoint is doing.

"Communities want to come in and hang out while they're getting messaged on marketing and branding," says Levinson of Cranial Tap. "The goal is for people to want to hang out amongst your messaging."

If yours is a business-to-business service, then you might dispense with the café and go the AssociationWorks route: All your traffic will be there because you're hosting meetings that are on the calendars of the people behind the avatars, not because they're looking for a place to hang out.

2. Know How Much You Want to Spend

Even though you can get into Second Life for a cost that's low by the standards of some of your Internet initiatives, don't undercut yourself. Although you can get some pretty sophisticated applications off the shelf for very little money, if you have something very specific in mind, a custom build might be the only way you can go.

"A lot of stuff you have to make from scratch," says Williams of MojoZoo. "Sometimes you can't find anything that's exactly what you need or you find something that's close and—this happens a lot in Second Life—you try to contact the creator, and the creator's long gone, or it's under a different account, so you're stuck. Another problem is broken vendors. Sometimes you'll want to buy something, and the vendor is malfunctioning, so you send a message to the builder, and they don't respond. Or the vendor might be from another country, so you might face a language barrier." (Note: The platform's instant messaging tool provides for automatic translation in a number of foreign languages, so you can override that limitation somewhat in some cases.)

Going into a project with an understanding that you can use a mix of custom-built and off-the-shelf objects and applications is helpful as you plan your budget. As we've seen in some of our examples, off-the-shelf objects and applications are highly affordable for now: You can probably obtain and outfit an entire office for a few hundred dollars, including costs for buying or leasing your space. Your costs escalate when you start getting into custom programming for applications, and, in these cases, you're starting to look at a pricing structure that's close to what you pay for custom Web development.

Thus you need to decide if you're going to be in for a few hundred dollars, in which case you're limited to off-the-shelf inventory, or a custom or semicustom build, in which case you're looking at potentially thousands of dollars, and hundreds of thousands of dollars in highly sophisticated projects that involve lots of complex programming and lots of space.

3. Find Yourself a Developer or Marketing Consultant

Developers and marketing consultants are not interchangeable, but many real-life and in-world specialists do both; they just come at it from different points of view. A developer is a programmer, someone who can make your objects and do your scripting for your animations and applications. Developers who know the environment, though, are good resources for learning about the rhythms of the platform, too, and in that sense they can function as a marketing consultant for you.

Marketing pros who know this space also typically do programming. If they don't, they know developers who might make a good fit for you. Either way, you want to work with these professionals to get you started on the right foot. In Appendix B, you'll find a list, necessarily selective, of developers and marketing pros who know the environment. I've tried to include a sample size that's both manageable—just a dozen or so—and somewhat representative. It's just a starting point.

4. Determine the Where and the What of Your Space

When working with your developer or consultant, determine whether to locate in a PG or a mature area, keeping in mind the strengths and weaknesses of each, and then design your space with how to leverage your product or service accordingly. Should your space be exciting or tranquil? If you're selling motorcycles, it will be exciting; if you're facilitating meetings, it will be tranquil. As part of this, be clear on who your neighbors are. There's only rudimentary zoning in Second Life, so to a certain extent, residents don't give it a second thought if there's a law firm office next to a strip club. But since you have your brand equity to protect, it might be in your interest despite residents' nonchalance about your neighbors to factor in the character of your neighborhood as you make your choices. One tactic to consider is setting up on a whole island, as Williams recommends to his clients. That way you have total control. Also, plan your space with current grid capacity issues in mind. If you want to host more than 50 people at a time on a regular basis, consider having two or three spaces located in different sims. That way you can have three meetings simultaneously, or, if you can get it, space at the intersection of multiple sims.

5. Market Your Space in a Way That Makes Sense

If yours is a business-to-business enterprise, clearly you don't need to market. All your visitors are attending by invitation. If you're consumer-oriented and want to attract traffic, there are several vehicles at your disposal: (1) the in-house search engine, which lists sites by category (special events, places, etc.) and hierarchically (by traffic numbers); (2) the in-house classified ads, which list sites hierarchically based on the advertising spend; (3) in-world marketing venues, like billboards and kiosks; (4) in-world publications; and (5) avatar-to-avatar communications.

Fees for all these options are denominated in depressed Linden dollars, so you're generally talking about costs that are not that high, maybe the equivalent of a few dollars. But in some categories fees can get significant because you're, in effect, bidding against others. If you want your site to come up first under, say, the services category and the current high bidder is paying the equivalent of $400 to come up first in the category, then you have to decide what being first is worth to you. It might be worth $10 but not $400. Your option in a case like this is to advertise in a different category where the top bidder isn't so high, but depending on your product or service, moving to a lower-cost category might make little sense.

Avatar-to-avatar communications is an option that doesn't have much of a model in the real world. Among other things, you can create an avatar and include information about your site in the information that other avatars see, or you can build that information into the avatar's name, something on the order of what DietAdvisor Vella has done: she keeps her name, DietAdvisor Vella, floating above her head at all times, so avatars instantly know what she's all about. In other cases, you can add a bit of information to the avatar's identity. For example, you might hire an avatar to display certain information at certain times, in a format that approximates something like this: John Doe (ABC Café Marketing Director). The moniker is an open invitation to anyone who's interested to learn more about the café as the avatar scoots around the platform chatting up people.

6. Be in It for the Long Haul

Yes, the platform has a lot of challenges to work through on the technical side, and yes, the traffic figures might not be what you want yet, but you're on the ground floor of an entirely new medium. Other social 3-D platforms are in the works. As competition heats up, you can bet on improved, more intuitive interfaces for participants and enhanced performance on the pesky problems like lag and grid capacity for your computer.

Without requiring too great a leap of imagination, you can see where all this is going: a direct link to the World Wide Web, so that from your Web site you can send your customers directly to the social, 3-D features of a platform like Second Life and then back again to your Web site. Thus, if you're a real estate broker, you can send home shoppers to Second Life for an avatar, as Coldwell Banker has done, and then send them to a 3-D model. That's not too different from what most brokers are already enabling shoppers to do today, although they are using video virtual tours instead of 3-D ones. The 3-D tours that link from your Web site aren't that far down the road.

Coldwell Banker has already mapped one way to do it. So, technically, all the pieces are in place for that to happen now on a substantial scale; it's just not practical and cost-effective yet for every broker to get into doing that. So, the issue is really when, not whether, to do it. That's why you want your foray into Second Life to be paid for in patient, not anxious, dollars.

THE BOTTOM LINE

Second Life is a platform of unusual depth, the product of tens of thousands of individual users who've created the hodgepodge of lands that comprise it today. As was mentioned earlier, although commercial activity has long been a part of the experience, much of the early days of the platform were developed by communities with noncommercial activities in mind. So, role-playing societies remain a big part of the experience and contribute to the platform's complex mosaic. The pure-play in-world businesses remain another very large part of what's going on, and although we're seeing the emergence of models that point the way to making money for products and services denominated only in Linden dollars, this in-world economy has some way to go before it matures. Most money-making ventures are very basic in nature: real estate and retail sales mostly, and also adult businesses, including clubs.

It's in this context that you're building a presence for your business, and it is the intent of this book to bring a few of the thoughts of the early adopters to you so you can start your planning process with a little bit of their insight, just enough to help you start generating ideas. What you've seen is that the platform remains new and is only now being tested vigorously, so that all you can reasonably hope for at this point is, if you're a consumer company, a marketing boost to your brand with a fairly select global community of young, tech-savvy people, but one that's gradually expanding to attract the consumer mainstream. And if you're a nonprofit organization or a business-to-business company, you're provided with a promising platform for hosting meetings and employing novel ways to exchange information, brainstorm, and collaborate on projects.

What you can hope for tomorrow is quite a bit more: an entirely new way of doing business and interacting with others. But you have to be on the platform to leverage that new reality as it matures.

PUTTING IT ALL TOGETHER: ONE SAMPLE APPROACH

Any move onto the platform must start with that first step, the introductory memo that lays out your rationale for, and approach to, taking the plunge. To give you an idea of how you might approach it, here's a sample memo articulating the how and the why for one landscaping company's move into Second Life.

AA-Green Yard Landscaping Company

Memorandum

To: John Executive
From: Bill Project-Manager
Re: Our use of Second Life: ideas and numbers

The 3-D virtual platform Second Life provides a number of compelling opportunities for delivering content to our landscaping professionals and our customers in a uniquely effective, and surprisingly cost-effective, way for our company. Here are a few thoughts.

What we can do

First, I want to suggest we maintain a virtual office with a conference room, training center, and landscaping lab (mock residential yard and commercial grounds), all of which would include capabilities for presenting PowerPoint slides and video, and uploading documents, and would be fully voice-enabled, allowing for conversations on top of text-based instant messaging. This location would function as our permanent base and would be directly accessible from our Web sites via what's known as a SLURL (a Second Life URL). It could also be made password protected to prohibit access by avatars without invitation. (We could also maintain a publicly accessible space for marketing and other types of outreach.) By creating access via our Web sites using the SLURL, we solve two major problems that are often cited as weaknesses of the Second Life platform:

1. We make it almost seamless for people unfamiliar with the platform to get directly to our location, eliminating the need for them to invest time in learning how to navigate.

2. We enable participants to bypass objectionable areas.

I say direct access would be almost seamless, but there would still be a bump to get over for platform neophytes, and I talk about that in more detail elsewhere. That said, with this setup, we would be enabled to host interactive presentations for our landscaping professionals and our consumers in the following way.

Using the training center, we can host experts to talk about subjects that lend themselves to a classroom setting. In a session for our landscaping professionals, for example, we can have an attorney talk about ways to avoid lawsuits by unhappy customers. In a session for consumers, we can have a landscaping professional talk about invasive insects that can ruin a yard.

Using the landscaping lab, we can host outside experts to discuss and demonstrate matters involving landscaping best practices. In a session for our own landscaping professionals, for example, we can host an arborist on different types of small trees and their favored climates and care. By using a preprogrammed control board, the expert can show different trees or the same tree infested with different invasive insect species. In a session for consumers, we can host one of our own professionals to discuss and display different arrangements of trees and bushes to maximize summer shade.

Using the conference room, we can host a meeting of our division managers, in which setting speakers can provide Power-Point slides, video, or any other audiovisual presentation available in a regular meeting setting.

How much it would cost

For a permanent, branded setting (under a 12-month lease arrangement), developed and maintained by a professional 3-D development company, annual cost would be an estimated $3,000. For this amount we'd get a stand-alone office building with a conference room, classroom space, and our landscaping lab, all located on a password-protected site on what's known as a class 5 server, which would allow us to host up to more than 50 people at a time. (Older servers have a capacity problem, making it difficult to host more than 30-40 people without creating significant lag, which is a delay in downloading time.)

There are less expensive ways to do this. For example, we could rent an auditorium for as little as $100 whenever we wanted to host a presentation, or we could simply buy a landscaped plot of land for, say, $700 on another owner's island (16-acre "sim" of virtual land) and have it available for presentations. But taking either of these approaches is work-intensive and potentially problem-plagued. First, it would be logistically burdensome not to have a permanent, password-protected area to which we could maintain direct access through our own unique SLURL. Second, we would have to rely on our own tech support for video and PowerPoint downloads, any preprogramming for demonstrations (like changing tree samples) or else pay extra to hire third-party tech help on a case-by-case basis. Third, we would face other ancillary costs and staff time for anything beyond the basics. For example, for an invasive-species presentation, we'd have to invest time and money in finding and acquiring different tree types, or, as I mentioned earlier, bringing on board someone to program the different types from scratch. Fourth, depending on the deal we work out, we'd face higher costs for protected facilities and for facilities on the highest-class server to get optimal performance. So, over a 12-month period, if we hosted, say, four events, we could quickly find much of the savings evaporated.

Clearly, forming a relationship with a professional development company is a gold-plated option, but it minimizes investment in staff effort and enables us to focus on what we want to do rather than on how to proceed. At the same time, the in-world presentations can be organized as revenue-generating by opening up the events to other, noncompeting companies as advertising or sponsorship opportunities. A single, $3,000-sponsor of four quarterly seminars on home staging, for example, would offset our development costs while giving the sponsor a novel, ground-breaking advertising opportunity.

What some real-world hurdles are

For all its potential, Second Life remains a challenging medium. To access it, people need fairly new computers, and navigation isn't immediately intuitive. Yet there are ways to minimize these challenges so that people in general can quickly benefit from participating in a real-time, virtual presentation in an interactive 3-D environment.

Here's how we might do it:

1. We maintain two standing links on our Web site. The first link goes to the new accounts page on Second Life's Web site, and the second goes to our permanent in-world location.

2. Once we plan an event for a particular audience, we set ourselves a limit (say, 40 participants) and then market the event through our usual channels (our Web page, our consumer newsletter, and our point-of-sale brochures). As part of the marketing, we direct people to our Web site for directions on participation and registration.

3. The directions on participation walk registrants through the new-account process. Using the link, they go directly to Second Life, where they open up a free account (it takes just a few minutes) and are directed to leave their new Second Life browser open and return to our site, where they access the SLURL. We recommend that they access our site at any time prior to the presentation to familiarize themselves with navigation and return at the designated time for the presentation.

4. At the time of presentation, they return to our Web site to click on the SLURL to get transported to the in-world location, and the presentation takes place.

5. Prior to the presentation, we would prepare the person hosting the show the same way we would any other presentation but with the added preparation for the person to get acclimated to the platform.

Under this scenario, it's possible for someone who's never been on the platform to attend a presentation with minimal investment in time and effort. Clearly, this isn't a seamless process, but neither is it that much more challenging for a person than participating in a webinar for the first time.

Here are the benefits

There are some genuinely unique ways to leverage this environment. For example, showing different ways to landscape a yard, instantly, in 3-D space while interacting in real-time with people in different locations, is not something that's easily done in any other type of environment. Although you can display different landscaping scenarios using 3-D graphical images with multiple people over the Internet, there remain some things you can't do without a 3-D platform. For example, you can't concurrently enable each participant to view the images from different angles, which is something you can do in Second Life, where, at any time, participants can change their orientation to the house. They can decide whether they want to look at it from above or behind, from the inside or from one of the exterior sides, and how frequently to change their orientation. What's more, depending on how you set up the presentation, they can control the variations on the house.

At the same time, participants at any time can communicate with the group as a whole or privately one-on-one, move about the platform at will, and, if the programming allows, create their own objects. All of these combine to make the environment potentially interactively richer than what's available on the Internet.

Given that consumers and even other landscaping companies are starting to embrace this platform, we would be providing value to our landscaping professionals and to our consumer base by leveraging this unique environment to bring them educational and other value-rich experiences they otherwise wouldn't have. In the process, we enhance our brand with consumers by giving them value-added service, increase the skill of our professionals, create revenue-generating opportunities, and present a cutting-edge face to an increasingly tech-savvy clientele.

WHAT *HARVARD BUSINESS REVIEW* THINKS OF ALL THIS

In the course of doing research for this book, a few articles stood out for their strength in capturing key aspects of what's important about Second Life's platform and what it holds for the future—or what the future holds for it. Unlike the bulk of the articles on which I relied to learn about what's going on, most of which were news articles, these few articles are thought pieces and raise issues you'll need to consider as you decide what to do, or even whether to do anything, in the brave new world of virtual platforms.

Given the value of these thought pieces, it's beneficial to you to have them reproduced here in their entirety, and so I've done that for two articles, starting with this piece by Paul Hemp in the June 2006 issue of *Harvard Business Review*. The article looks at the future of marketing for product brands like Coca-Cola and Adidas in virtual environments. While it focuses on Second Life as the most advanced environment, it looks at the whole panoply of virtual worlds.

In its essence, the article describes a picture in which marketing efforts by the big brands will indeed change the nature of virtual environments, but probably more important, the virtual environments will ultimately change the nature of marketing. And it's how marketing will change that you need to have on your radar screen. As a side note, some of the Second Life statistics Hemp includes in the piece will differ from ones I've included in earlier chapters, and those differences simply reflect the growth of the platform from the time he did his writing and the time I did mine; the statistics will be still different by the time you read this because of the platform's rapid growth.

Avatar-Based Marketing

BY PAUL HEMP

Take a minute—go ahead, don't be timid—to step into the strange but compelling virtual world of Second Life. The landscape of brown hills is dotted with often-fantastic buildings—some homes, some businesses—and a tantalizing array of information kiosks, drivable vehicles, and fanciful interactive objects just waiting to be investigated.

Birdsong and a gentle breeze enliven the scene at dawn, and as you walk by a house later in the day you may hear music emanating from an open window. When people approach you to chat—their hands typing on an invisible keyboard to indicate that a line of dialogue will soon appear on your screen—their movements are slightly awkward. But these folks aren't android-like in appearance or in action: Their outfits are elaborate, and most of their gestures—a nod, a shrug, a beckoning arm—are quite realistic.

Some things in this virtual world may seem bizarre at first. Many residents wear sexually provocative clothing, and some inhabit an animal or other nonhuman body. The truly odd thing about this place, though? You're not you. In Second Life, you live in a new body and take on the identity of your "avatar"—that is, a being you've created as a representation of yourself in this online environment.

Avatars aren't the only personal creations in Second Life. Nearly everything in this world—which encompasses 50 virtual square miles and would take days to walk across, although you can save time by flying or by instantly teleporting yourself from one place to another—has been made by Second Life residents. Along with the thousands of eye-catching structures, physical landmarks, and interactive objects, these creations include less tangible things: virtual businesses, interest-based social groups, and scheduled events that range from dance parties to celebrity book signings to boxing matches to yard sales.

Clearly, many of Second Life's 100,000 or so residents are highly involved with this place. And that makes it potentially a dream marketing venue. Instead of targeting passive eyeballs, marketers here have the opportunity to interact with engaged minds. Commerce is already an integral part of Second Life. Residents spend—in Linden dollars, the local currency, available at in-world ATMs—the equivalent of $5 million a month on resident-to-resident transactions for in-world products and services. Certainly, introducing real-world brands, in some form or another, is a logical next step.

But wait. Whom do your marketing efforts target? The flesh-and-blood Second Life members who gave their credit card numbers to register for the game—or their Second Life avatars residing in the virtual world? Sure, the real-world human controls the real-world wallet. The avatar, though, arguably represents a distinctly different "shadow" consumer, one able to influence its creator's purchase of real-world products and conceivably make its own real-world purchases in the virtual world. At the least, it may offer insights into its creator's hidden tastes.

Such questions aren't academic. Second Life is just one of a growing number of three-dimensional virtual worlds, accessible via the Internet, in which users, through an avatar, are able to play games or simply interact socially with thousands of people simultaneously. By some estimates, more than 10 million people spend $10 to $15 a month to subscribe to online role-playing environments, with the number of subscribers doubling every year. Millions more enter free sites, some of them sponsored by companies as brand-building initiatives. Many users spend upward of 40 hours a week in these worlds. And as the technology improves over the next decade, virtual worlds may well eclipse film, TV, and non–role-playing computer games as a form of entertainment. That's because, instead of watching someone else's story unfold in front of them on a screen, users in these worlds create and live out their own stories.

When marketing online, "you want sustained engagement with the brand rather than just a click-through" to a purchase or product information, says Bonita Stewart, responsible for interactive marketing for DaimlerChrysler's Jeep, Chrysler, and Dodge brands. "Avatars create an opportunity for just this type of engagement."

Given the potential, marketers need to acquaint themselves with the phenomenon of avatars and to consider whether it requires a rethinking of marketing messages and channels. They can draw on the experiences of the handful of pathfinding companies that have begun to explore this realm.

What Is an Avatar?

People have long taken on alternative identities, from authors' sly noms de plume to CB [citizens' band] radio operators' evocative handles to chat-room visitors' sexually suggestive user names. But in the last few years, technology has expanded the possibilities. Today, a teenager will communicate in the voice of two personae—one transmitted over cell phone and the other via instant messaging—to the same friend at the same time. An unattractive, shy man will transform himself into the sexiest and most aggressive guy—or, not uncommonly, girl—on the virtual block. A Web surfer may change her persona every time she enters one of the hundreds of three-dimensional chat rooms. Like the ancient rite of the bal masqué, modern technology helps people realize a deepseated desire to experience what it would feel like to be someone else. In the words of a famous New Yorker cartoon showing man's best friend sitting at a computer screen: "On the Internet, nobody knows you're a dog."

The avatar is the most conspicuous online manifestation of people's desire to try out alternative identities or project some private aspect of themselves. (The word, which originally described the worldly incarnation of the Hindu god Vishnu, was popularized in its cybersense by Neal Stephenson in his 1992 cult novel *Snow Crash*.) Broadly defined, "avatar" encompasses not only complex beings created for use in a shared virtual reality but any visual representation of a user in an online community. For example, more than 7 million people have created Yahoo avatars, simple but personalized cartoonlike characters used as pictorial signatures in activities ranging from instant messaging to fantasy sports.

The experience of living through an alternative self is the most powerful, though, in virtual worlds, sometimes called— take a breath—massively multiplayer online role-playing games. In these environments, someone's avatar, or "av," can evolve from a being created using standard character and appearance options initially offered to new users into a unique and richly developed individual. Avatars are endowed with mannerisms, skills, and wardrobes that their users create (employing a variety of software tools), purchase (from in-world shops), receive as gifts (from other avatars), or earn (through in-game achievements). Indeed, while avatars' anonymity is part of their appeal, many people take considerable pride in their creations as public expressions of hidden aspects of their identities. Those who don't have the time or desire to enhance their avatars on their own spend a combined total of more than $100 million a year on Internet auction sites for skills and accessories—digital weapons earned or crafted by others, for example—that can improve their avatars' presence and performance in a particular world.

Movies are even made in these worlds, using computer game technology, a form of filmmaking dubbed "machinima." Avatars take on scripted roles, thus creating in these plays within plays characters that are two steps removed from their real-life creators. You might call them avatars' avatars.

The online worlds populated by avatars come in many forms but can basically be divided into two types. The most popular by far are combat-focused games, such as EverQuest, Lineage, and World of Warcraft: The latter alone claims more than 6 million paying subscribers. Other virtual worlds, even if they include game-like elements, primarily offer the opportunity for social interaction. In these worlds—places like Second Life and Entropia Universe, aimed at adults, and the more teen-oriented There, the Sims Online, and Habbo Hotel—users customize not only themselves but also their environments and experiences, decorating personal living spaces or running their own events. The settings are more realistic than those in the typical sci-fi or fantasy combat game. Though you often need to pay a monthly subscription to get the full experience—to buy your own land in Second Life, for instance, or to sell virtual items you've made in There—the operators of many of these social virtual worlds recently have allowed people to join and explore the worlds for free. This approach has boosted the sites' membership numbers. Second Life currently has around 65,000 paying subscribers and another 100,000 nonpaying members with fewer in-world privileges, according to Linden Lab, the company that developed and runs that world.

In such worlds, people often have more than one avatar. And these can differ substantially from one another and from the creator's public self. Gender switching is common, as is the exaggeration of sexual characteristics. Some of these worlds have communities of nonhuman avatars—for example, "furries," animal-like beings that often reflect their real-life creators' strong psychological associations with certain animal types. One Second Life avatar, a well-muscled and spiky-haired male named wilde Cunningham, represents a group of people who are severely physically disabled in real life. And avatars can take on lives of their own: Because of real-world news reports about their virtual-world activities as community gadflies or wealthy entrepreneurs, avatars sometimes become better known than their creators.

Living in the skin of an avatar—looking out through its eyes and engaging with other beings, themselves avatars of flesh-and-blood individuals—can be an intense experience. Though in most worlds avatars don't eat, sleep, or use the bathroom, serious relationships are formed—avatars adopt avatar children, numerous virtual-world relationships lead to real-world marriages—and land ownership sparks sometimes nasty disputes over property rights. Put it all together and you have an avatar that is "not a puppet but a projection" of some aspect of the creator's self, says Philip Rosedale, founder and CEO of Linden Lab.

Marketing in virtual worlds

The real-world marketing potential of online worlds is suggested by the active virtual commerce that already takes place within them. In Second Life, for instance, you find services you might expect—virtual clothing and furniture design, event planning, real estate brokering. But the avatar-run businesses also include detective agencies, which keep an eye on virtual infidelity; a notary public, who guarantees the legitimacy of avatar contracts (and offers mediation services if problems arise); and an advertising agency, which designs and places ads for other avatar-operated businesses. There are in addition the inevitable sex shops, which sell not only racy garb and paraphernalia but also computer code that allows two avatars to enter into a passionate embrace and beyond.

Second Life residents pay for these products and services in local Linden dollars. Merchants can then exchange them, at fluctuating rates, for real-world cash on various Internet exchanges. Some avatar entrepreneurs, most notably fashion designers and land speculators, have been so successful that their creators have quit real-life jobs to focus on their virtual-world businesses. Linden Lab says that more than 3,000 people earn real-world money from their Second Life businesses, averaging $20,000 a year—a number skewed upward by the handful of residents who generate six-figure incomes in real-world dollars.

The line between virtual and real worlds is blurring in other ways. In Second Life, perhaps the most technologically advanced of these environments, the BBC recently broadcast a segment of its Newsnight program from within the world. Internet intellectual property expert Lawrence Lessig gave a speech to a full house and electronically signed virtual copies of his latest book. A proliferation of "Impeach Bush" signs— that were installed by an avatar on tiny plots of land he had purchased, blocking many people's views—created an uproar.

Furthermore, many residents import real-world company logos as props or decorations. Coke machines are common. You can buy a Corona beer at a Second Life bar while listening to the hum of a neon Budweiser sign from the wall. Evian was advertised at the concession stand of a recent U2 tribute concert. An iPod store sells virtual players loaded with tunes audible when your avatar wears one of the devices, and a store called Pear sells a laptop that sends e-mails to the real world and bears a fruit-shaped logo reminiscent of Apple Computer's.

The combination of robust virtual-world commerce and the growing overlap of virtual worlds and the real world suggest opportunities for creative real-world marketers. So far, there have been few instances of real-world products being sold in virtual worlds to real-world users for delivery to their real-world addresses. But there have been some interesting brand-building experiments. In the Sims Online, McDonald's installed virtual fast-food kiosks, complete with automated employees working at the counter and able to serve up (free) virtual burgers and fries to residents who made their selections from a clickable menu. Intel incorporated its logo into the screens of virtual computers that, when purchased by Sims Online residents (using "simoleans," the in-world currency), helped them improve their game skills. In the virtual world There, Levi Strauss promoted a new style of jeans by offering virtual versions for sale to avatars, pricing them (in "ThereBucks") at a premium to the generic virtual jeans that avatars otherwise could purchase. Nike sold virtual shoes that allowed wearers to run faster than other avatars.

Organizations have also sponsored branded events in virtual worlds. For example, Kellogg's sponsored a competition, in the teen-oriented world of Habbo Hotel, in which residents were asked to decorate their personal rooms in various Pop-Tart–related themes. (The winner received a room filled with rare in-game Habbo items, such as a DJ deck and a beehive-shaped lamp, that couldn't be purchased by users in the Habbo furnishings catalog.) In a noncommercial sponsorship, the American Cancer Society staged its "Relay for Life" event in Second Life. Resident avatars walked a virtual course, lighted virtual luminaries, and raised virtual cash, which was converted into more than $5,000 in real cash and donated to the organization.

There obviously is a real danger that product placement in virtual worlds will feel to residents like three-dimensional spam. To be effective, marketing in these worlds needs to be consistent with the virtual environment and enhance partici-pants' experience. "You don't want to simply shove a billboard in people's face," says Betsy Book, editor of the Virtual Worlds Review Web site and director of product management for There. "You want a brand to be integrated into the daily rou-tines of potential customers so that they can, if they choose, interact with it in a meaningful way." In that sense, campaigns like those for Levi's and Nike represented successful virtual-world placements, she says. Moreover, the Nike initiative, by helping in-world wearers to run faster, had the added benefit of heightening the user's virtual-world experience.

Companies have also created entirely branded virtual worlds—"adverworlds," Book calls them. Wells Fargo bank recently launched Stagecoach Island, which is designed to educate teens about money matters through games and so-cial activities. The branding is low-key: The Wells Fargo name is almost absent, appearing most conspicuously at the ATMs where players take a financial quiz in order to withdraw vir-tual cash for activities such as skydiving and paintball games. However, subtle brand building through education rather than the peddling of financial services is the intention, says

Tim Collins, the bank's senior vice president for experience marketing. "An educated consumer is our best customer," he says. For that reason, the company may tinker with the ratio between fun and financial education—"currently about 99 to 1," jokes Collins—in the next version of the game. In a similar vein, DaimlerChrysler has a site for preteens called Mokitown, a cartoonlike world designed to educate players—called "mokis," short for "mobile kids"—about road and traffic safety through a shared social experience.

Coca-Cola's Coke Studios is another teen-oriented world in which nearly everything from the furniture to the vending machines that dispense miniature Cokes are branded or bear the company's red and white colors. Avatars—known as "v-egos," which stands for virtual egos—accumulate points ("decibels") in public studios through various music-related activities. For example, you get five decibels when a fellow avatar likes the mix of music you have selected as a virtual DJ. (You get ten points when you drink a virtual Coke.) V-egos use these points to buy furniture for their studios, where they can hold events for avatar friends. "Teens desire not only to experience things but also to express themselves," says Doug Rollins, the Coke brand manager who oversees Coke Studios, which claims 8 million registered users. These players spend an average of 40 minutes at the free site when they visit, he says—the kind of engagement that is invaluable in building a brand.

So far, real-world marketing initiatives in virtual worlds are rare. The customer base is still small—visitors to the Coke Studios site at a given time typically number only in the hundreds—and marketers are still unfamiliar with the new medium and skeptical about what it can offer. Patrice Varni, head of Internet marketing for Levi's, says the 2003 campaign in which residents of There outfitted themselves in the company's virtual jeans was an interesting experiment but one she had hoped would yield more data—how many people were willing to pay extra for Levi's versus generic jeans, for example, or what avatars did when they were wearing Levi's. Technology is improving, though, and she can envision placements in which users could, by making an in-world purchase of an appealing style of jeans, effect a real-world online purchase.

In the meantime, there may be little to lose from experimenting. A company called Massive Incorporated, which sells real-world advertising in a network of computer games, recently signed a deal to place ads in the online virtual world Entropia Universe. In Second Life, where the world is a creation of the users, marketers can simply become residents and have their avatars try out marketing initiatives for free—something a number of companies are already quietly doing, according to David Fleck, vice president for marketing at Linden Lab. "People think they need to create a partnership with us, but all they have to do is join, go and buy a chunk of land, and then do what they want to do," says Fleck, pointing out that the company's business model is based on subscriptions and the sale of land and Linden dollars. "Making us an intermediary only creates friction in the process."

Marketing to Avatars

Advertising has always targeted a powerful consumer alter ego: that hip, attractive, incredibly popular person just waiting to emerge (with the help of the advertised product) from an all-too-normal self. Now that, in virtual worlds, consumers are taking the initiative and adopting alter egos that are anything but under wraps, marketers can segment, reach, and influence them directly. Indeed, it's important for companies to think about more than the potentially rich market of the virtual world and consider the potential customer—the avatar.

For starters, avatars are certainly useful subjects for market research. "Marketing depends on soliciting people's dreams," says Henry Jenkins, head of MIT's Comparative Media Studies program. "And here those dreams are on overt display." For instance, a company could track how inhabitants of a virtual world use or otherwise interact with a particular type of product, noting choices they make about product features, wardrobe mix, or even virtual vacation destinations.

It could then use those choices to create profiles of potential customer segments. For instance, in creating a Yahoo avatar, people choose from an array of elements, including physical features, accessories such as pets, and the setting in which the avatar appears. Some of these elements include branded items: Adidas shoes, say, or a Jeep Commander parked in the background. While encouraging avatars to wear real-world products is mainly aimed at enhancing the brand, even at this rudimentary level one could learn that avatars who choose golden retrievers as pets prefer Jeep Grand Cherokees over Jeep Commanders. As the options presumably multiply in the future, and the avatars become more complex, one could assemble detailed profiles of those who might be likely buyers of either kind of model.

Avatars might also be enlisted to play a marketing role. They could use their virtual-world sensibility to design products with real-world potential. Several Second Life clothing designers have been approached by real-world fashion houses, and at least one business makes real-world versions of furniture based on virtual "furni" designed by Second Life residents. Avatar brokers could link up real-world companies with virtual landowners willing to rent space for the companies' marketing initiatives. Avatars ultimately could run virtual-world stores selling real-world products or become what Internet culture blogger Tony Walsh calls "advertars," paid to publicize, overtly or not, those same products.

But will avatars actually buy real-world products that are marketed in virtual worlds, in effect purchasing real-world goods for their creators, just as those creators buy virtual-world paraphernalia for them? Could an avatar who currently spends Linden dollars to buy a virtual skirt from another avatar's designer clothing store in Second Life be enticed, while visiting an in-world Gap retail outlet, to click on a cash register and use his or her creator's credit card to buy a real-world Gap sweater that would be shipped to the creator's doorstep?

At the least, avatars are likely to window shop. Michael K. Wilson, CEO of Makena Technologies, which runs There, says that e-commerce sites, while they have reduced retailers' brick-and-mortar costs, don't address the inherently social nature of shopping, especially for women. But in the mall of a virtual world, an avatar could try on—and try out in front of virtual friends—real-world clothing brands or styles her creator typically couldn't afford or wouldn't dare to wear. If she got rave reviews from her pals and became (along with her creator) comfortable with the idea of wearing a particular outfit, a purchase in the real world might follow. "It doesn't cost anything for someone to create an individualized outfit, even mixing several brands," says Dave Kopp, head of community applications at Yahoo and manager of the company's avatar program. "And it doesn't cost anything for companies to supply the products that become part of this act of self-expression and personal brand endorsement."

The amount of marketing and purchasing data that could be mined is staggering. An avatar's digital nature means that every one of its moves—for example, perusing products in a store and discussing them with a friend—can be tracked and logged in a database. This behavioral information, organized by individual avatar, aside from being priceless to marketers in the long term, could be processed immediately. An avatar clerk might appear from behind the counter and offer to answer an avatar customer's questions—questions the clerk would already know because they would have been gathered and recorded in the database.

Furthermore, the avatar clerk might automatically adjust his or her behavior to become more appealing to the avatar customer. Research conducted at Stanford University's Virtual Human Interaction Lab has found that users are more strongly influenced by avatars who mimic their own avatars' body movements and mirror their own appearance. This virtual manifestation of an old sales trick makes avatars potentially, if insidiously, powerful salespeople. Using a simple computer script, the selling avatar clerk is able to subtly and automatically tailor its behavior—its gait, the way it turns its head, its facial features—to the avatar buyer's, thus making the clerk seem more friendly, interesting, honest, and persuasive.

Even more astonishing, digital technology allows avatar sellers to modify their behavior and appearance so that they simultaneously mimic the different gestures and look of hundreds of avatars in the same room—at least in the virtual eyes of each of those potential buyers. "If I want a group of virtual people to buy a product, I can morph my avatar to subtly act like every one of them," says Jeremy Bailenson, an assistant professor of communications at Stanford and the lab director.

So what is an avatar's perspective on buying real-world goods with real-world currency in virtual worlds? One afternoon in Second Life, Minxy Moe and her boyfriend Ben Stravinsky sit next to a rushing waterfall in the yard of their friend LadyLizzie Charming and talk with a visiting journalist (or rather, his avatar) about commercial incursions into their world. Minxy and Ben are skeptical about real-world marketing in Second Life, saying that people generally like to keep the two worlds separate. LadyLizzie echoes these sentiments. "I would not be caught dead in real life wearing the clothes I wear here," she says, glancing down at her revealing halter top, scanty shorts—and branded Adidas high-tops, which she purchased in Second Life.

"Maybe subliminal advertising might work," muses Minxy.

"It would be a large advertising budget wasted, in my opinion," says Ben.

LadyLizzie starts to warm to the idea of a Gap outlet in Second Life, before Ben interjects: "Without sounding harsh, clothes from the Gap are so boring," compared with Second Life attire.

Such anticommercial sentiments among avatars may be on the wane. Wagner James Au, one of a number of "embedded" journalists whose avatars post on the Internet regular dispatches from Second Life, says that, as Second Life has grown, purists fighting outside commercial influences have lost some of their clout. Two years ago, he wrote about an island in Second Life that was purchased by a British marketing company. The next day, sign-waving protesters picketed the island. Today, "a Starbucks—or whatever—isn't likely to generate that kind of acrimony," he says.

The potential of marketing directly to avatars doesn't disappear after they accompany their creators—tucked in their creators' psyches—back to the real world. A company might, for instance, create a real-world advertising campaign aimed at a particular avatar "segment"—wizards, say, or furries. Or you might offer in real-world stores a distinctive clothing line available only to people whose avatars had, through achievements in an online world, earned their creators the right to wear the gear, thus giving people credibility in the real world based on their avatars' virtual-world status. Marketers could thus "tie products to the game without busting the fantasy of the game itself," which is always a risk when marketing in virtual worlds, says Edward Castronova, a professor of telecommunications at Indiana University and the author of the 2005 book *Synthetic Worlds: The Business and Culture of Online Games*.

(By contrast, Walt Disney's Virtual Magic Kingdom site, instead of bestowing real-world credibility for what an avatar does online, grants virtual-world credibility for real-world activities. The site is designed to encourage visits to the company's real-world theme-park attractions. Avatars created at computer terminals in Disney's real-world amusement parks get to sport an exclusive "Born in Park" icon in the Virtual Magic Kingdom, giving them "Main Street cred," according to the Disney site.)

As the barriers between virtual worlds and real life blur, so do the barriers between virtual worlds and the rest of cyberspace. New technology allows a group of avatars, a "Web mob," to roam the Internet. Appearing as superimposed images on a Web page, they can check it out, make purchases if they feel like it, then zoom off as a group to other Web sites. Instead of having to seek out avatars in virtual worlds, savvy marketers may instead find ways to attract avatars to their e-commerce sites.

Real Challenges, Real Risks

This new marketing landscape and audience come with all kinds of pitfalls. There are technology constraints. Stagecoach Island moved from the technology platform on which Second Life is built to the platform underlying Active Worlds, another virtual world. The Second Life platform required too much computer hardware capability of users, according to Collins, the Wells Fargo marketer.

Strong resistance to real-world commercial encroachment still exists in many virtual worlds, where users primarily seek an escape from real life. In-world billboards, like those calling for Bush's impeachment, are occasionally defaced. And there was a mild though short-lived protest when MTV recently recruited avatars as models and sponsored a fashion show in Second Life, which was then aired on the network's broadband Internet channel, Overdrive.

It's also crucially important to realize that each virtual world has a different culture and people come to these worlds for a variety of reasons, so a single marketing approach won't work. Marketers should get to know a world they are thinking about entering. In the vast expanse of Second Life, there are

SELLING TO AVATARS— AND TO THEIR CREATORS

Online virtual worlds offer untapped marketing potential for real-world products and services, particularly because of their ability to generate sustained consumer engagement with a brand. This occurs through interactions with "avatars," the beings users create as representations of themselves and through which they live and relate to others in these worlds.

The stage for real-world marketing has been set in virtual worlds like Life. There, residents run businesses that sell virtual products and services priced in Second Life's Linden dollars, which are convertible into real-world currency on various Internet exchanges. In this example, Dominus Motors promotes a limited Eleanor edition (named after a famous 1960s muscle car) of its Shadow model that seats five avatars and can be driven through the world at speeds of up to 210 miles an hour.

Wells Fargo bank operates a virtual world called Stagecoach Island, designed to educate teens about money matters through games and social activities. At in-world ATMs, players take a financial quiz in order to withdraw virtual cash for activities such as skydiving and games of paintball.

Coke Studios is a teen-oriented virtual world run by Coca-Cola. In this world, users' avatars interact—that's conversation in the text boxes—and accumulate points through primarily music-related activities. For example, you get five decibels for each thumbs-up from a fellow avatar for your selection of dance music in your role as virtual DJ in one of the public studios. You can use these points to buy furniture and accessories for your own studio, where you can hold events for avatar friends.

nooks and crannies that may be viewed as a bit dicey by main-stream marketers—for instance, an island populated by Goreans, adherents of a series of fantasy novels by John Norman in which slavery and male domination of women are themes.

Consumers' privacy concerns about the detailed tracking of avatar data pose obvious challenges. So does the attempt to balance viral brand enhancement—many avatars on teen-age sites incorporate real-world brands into their user names—against the loss of brand control. Operators of virtual worlds make sporadic attempts to limit the unauthorized use of real-world brands, but even a company's intentional introduction of a brand into a virtual world can be risky: The McDonald's kiosks in the Sims Online, while popular, generated snigger-ing among residents about how fat the patrons would be-come, says Book, of Virtual Worlds Review.

Clearly, this is virtually unexplored marketing territory. But conceiving of avatars and other online personae as a new set of potential customers, one that can be analyzed and seg-mented, provides a useful way to think about new marketing opportunities. Indeed, the day may not be far off when some-one in a store—either virtual-world or real-world—says to a clerk, "Wait a minute. Let me have one of those as well. Af-ter all," the customer will add, in a near-echo of pregnant women's perennial refrain, "I'm buying for two."

Paul Hemp is a senior editor at *Harvard Business Review (HBR)* and the author of "Presenteeism: at Work—But Out of It" (*HBR*, October 2004) and "My Week as a Room-Service Waiter at the Ritz"

Reprinted with permission of *Harvard Business Review.*

IS A
TAX AUDIT
IN YOUR
FUTURE?

At the time I interviewed executives at Coldwell Banker about their virtual land, Ranchero, in mid-2007, just a few days after the company had hosted its launch event, its virtual "agents" had sold three virtual houses at $20 each (about 16,200 in Linden dollars). Now, I throw this question out to you: Is that $60 in income taxable?

I think it's a pretty good guess that if that $60 is never taken out of Second Life and instead remains denominated in virtual dollars as 16,200 Lindens, then there's a good chance that the U.S. government wouldn't expect that income to be declared on the company's tax forms. But then again, maybe it would. On the other hand, if the money is converted to U.S. dollars, then it seems reasonable that that money must be claimed. I'm not a tax expert, so I don't know what the real answer is. But even tax experts don't really know what the real answer is—yet.

Julian Dibbell, who's written a book about his quest to earn a living solely through his virtual gains, tackles the tax question in his book and also in the following January/February 2006 article in *Legal Affairs*, which I've reproduced in its entirety. The upshot is that the IRS isn't sure what to do, at least as of the time the article was written. But the article, which looks at platforms other than Second Life, is interesting for another reason: It shows, in the same way as the *Harvard Business Review* piece, just how big virtual worlds are becoming.

Dragon Slayers or Tax Evaders?

Buying and selling imaginary goods in computer-game worlds is big business. Now let's figure out whether gamers should pay real-world taxes on virtual treasures.

BY JULIAN DIBBELL

If you haven't misspent hours battling an Arctic Ogre Lord near an Ice Dungeon or been equally profligate spending time reading the published works of the Internal Revenue Service, you probably haven't wondered whether the United States government will someday tax your virtual winnings from games played over the Internet. The real question is, Why hasn't it happened already?

Gamers who play EverQuest, an online game with 450,000 subscribers—playing parts that range from Frogloks, a race of sentient amphibians, to Vah Shir, a regal feline race—generate in their virtual world the kind of imaginary economic activity that can be measured in real-world terms like "gross domestic product." According to Indiana University economist Edward Castronova, EverQuest's annual GDP—the total wealth in goods and services an economy creates—is about $135 million, or around half the GDP of the Caribbean island nation of Dominica. Castronova sized up the virtual economy (in a widely read 2001 paper that launched his career as the Adam Smith of video games) in part to mock the pomposity of traditional econometrics. But the finding of the paper was no joke. EverQuest's subscribers are playing a game, to be sure, yet like all massively multiplayer online games, often called MMOs, it's one with remarkable economic potential.

To play an MMO is to engage in a quest. You take a character into a virtual world to hunt monsters, seek treasure, and enjoy the thrill of slowly rising from humble beginnings to imaginary wealth and stature. The rub, however, is that you can rise only so far without finding treasures placed in the virtual world by the game's creators or acquiring those items from other players. There are various ways to convince your playmates to surrender their weapons, magic spells, and mineral ores. Killing their characters is one way and befriending them another, but the quickest method is to offer fellow gamers real money. This is rarely approved by official rules of MMOs, but the practice is so widespread that if you look on online marketplaces like eBay today, you will find a thriving, multimillion-dollar market in Golden Runic Hammers, Ethereal Mounts, and similarly exotic items—all of them won (and anything found or wrested from another player is "won" in the context of a game) or bartered for in this or that MMO quest, and many of them fetching prices in the hundreds, even thousands of dollars.

June 2003. I set myself the following challenge, posting it on my Web log for the world to see: "On April 15, 2004, I will truthfully report to the IRS that my primary source of income is the sale of imaginary goods—and that I earn more from it, on a monthly basis, than I have ever earned as a professional writer."

In the course of this project, I made a total of $11,000 selling on eBay the items I won playing a game called Ultima Online, $3,900 of which was in the final, most profitable month. I reported my profit to the IRS, and I paid the requisite taxes. But after I did so, a troublesome set of questions continued to nag at me—for which even IRS publication 525, entitled "Taxable and Nontaxable Income," couldn't provide answers.

This was remarkable, for publication 525 would appear to contain every conceivable form of income known to accounting. To read it once is to realize that you know nothing about income. Here you'll find a description of gains, ill-gotten and otherwise, so irregular that they can be taxed only according to that form of guesswork known as fair market value. Here are stocks, options, retirement watches, and stolen goods ("If you steal property, you must report its fair market value in your income in the year you steal it unless in the same year, you return it to its rightful owner").

Most significant for my purposes, here too are items acquired either through barter or as prizes in a game. The rules make clear the IRS's fundamental point: Goods taken in trade or won at play are taxable the moment they fall into somebody's hands, even if they are not sold for money. The more I read, the more I wondered whether reporting the amount I had brought home from selling virtual items on eBay was enough to satisfy the IRS.

What about the assets I bartered for or won in the game but never sold in the real world, the suits of armor stashed here and there with their easily established fair market value? What if I traded those assets for their value in Ultima Online's official currency, the Britannian gold piece, rather than for dollars? Wouldn't it be easy to establish their value in dollars nonetheless and, if I owed American taxes on the exchange, put a number on the deal that the IRS could grasp and love? And what about all the other MMO players out there—how long could the IRS be expected in good conscience to leave the resulting millions of dollars in wealth untouched?

You might think that I was letting my imagination run away with me—I certainly hoped I was. I thought that a glance at past IRS practices would assure me that the feds would never dream of taxing assets that had not been turned into money. I thought wrong.

The IRS has taxed barter transactions that are remarkably similar to the ones that online players engage in every day. In the late 1970s, for example, dozens of so-called barter clubs sprang up around the U.S., said Deborah Schenk, a tax professor at New York University School of Law. The clubs put out directories in which members listed themselves as providing accounting, window washing, or other types of services. Any member could buy those services with "trade dollars," a virtual currency like Britannian gold pieces, and a member could earn trade dollars by offering his own services. By 1980 these clubs were handling an estimated $200 million worth of transactions every year, and the IRS took notice. In a 1980 ruling, the agency said that barter club transactions produced taxable income, even though no actual money changed hands. A 1982 law made enforcement of the ruling easier by requiring the clubs to provide the IRS with information about every transaction.

Swapping a financial audit for a dental checkup seems different from trading a Runic Hammer for an Ethereal Mount, if only because audits and checkups are real. But what does "real" mean for tax purposes? Richard Schmalbeck, a tax professor at Duke University School of Law, said the IRS determines that something has "real" value when a similar good or service trades on a market for actual money. Transactions involving items with real value are taxable. He acknowledged, though, that not every situation is clear.

Schmalbeck described the case of David Zarin, a gambler who spent close to a year playing craps in a casino, essentially without leaving the casino. Zarin lost $3.4 million worth of chips he acquired on house credit and he converted few, if any, into actual money. Unable to collect, the casino wrote off all but $500,000 of his debt, arguably presenting Zarin with a gift of $2.9 million. Was that taxable, as the IRS claimed? Schmalbeck said that several courts reached different conclusions, unable to agree on whether the gambling debt or the gift (or, perhaps, the gambler's year in the casino) was real in any meaningful sense, even though the chips had fallen where they did and had a monetary value.

In any case, with virtual goods from Internet games being traded every day for actual money on eBay, wouldn't Schmalbeck's theory about similar goods trading on actual markets mean that trades occurring exclusively in a game are taxable? I set out for my local tax office in South Bend, Ind., to find out.

Arriving near the end of the workday, I took a chair until my number was called, and then approached the help desk, where a tax official named John Knight looked up at me with a mix of weariness and curiosity. I took a deep breath and proceeded to describe my business and the economy that sustained it. I cited publication 525. I inquired about barter income, specifically the difference, if any, between a painting for which the owner paid $6,000 bartered for half a year's rent and a virtual castle with a value of $1,200 established on eBay bartered for 10 million pieces of virtual gold. If John Knight's response was typical, the IRS hasn't done much thinking about the matter.

"O.K., so I got a fake jewel that's worth 80 million points, gives me all kinds of invincibility," said Knight, striving doggedly to nail down what I was talking about. "But I got two of them, or don't want to play [anymore]. And I can go on eBay and sell my jewel to some other character?"

"Uh, yeah," I confirmed.

Knight considered the facts and offered a nonbinding opinion: "That's so weird."

He ventured to say that it was doubtful the IRS would treat virtual items as cash equivalents anytime soon. Until the Britannian gold piece trades on international money markets, or until the value of a virtual amulet is as widely recognized as that of a beer, he suggested, "I don't think we're recognizing Dungeon and Dragon [sic] currency as legal tender."

Because he wasn't in a position to offer a final word, however, Knight gave me a number for the IRS's Business and Specialty Tax Line. "Specialty" sounded about right, so I called and told my story to a telereceptionist, who routed me to a small-business specialist, who passed me along to a barter-income specialist, who identified herself as "Mrs. Clardy, badge number 7500416," and listened in silence to my query about virtual economics—and then put me on hold.

When Mrs. Clardy returned, she was a bureaucrat transformed. "We just had this little discussion," she said, almost giggling. "And it sounds to us like [the online trades you've described] would be—yes—Internet barter." Here she paused, whether to catch her breath or to let the conclusion sink in, I couldn't tell. "However," she went on, "there are no regs, there is no code, there are no rulings, to rely upon. This is our opinion."

Mrs. Clardy suggested I seek a more authoritative judgment. A "private letter ruling," she assured me, was the IRS's definitive opinion, in writing, on a particular taxpayer's situation. And a letter ruling in my case, she believed, would probably be the closest the IRS had ever come to an opinion on the status of virtual income.

"The ramifications are enormous," Mrs. Clardy exhorted. "Break new ground!"

Why not? Well, because Mrs. Clardy had neglected to mention the $650 fee stipulated in the letter-ruling request instructions, or the tax lawyer I would have to hire to write the request with any effectiveness, or the six months I would have to wait for a final response. Even if none of these obstacles had stood in the way, I finally had to ask myself: Was this really the kind of ground I wanted to break?

Considering what the IRS had done with barter clubs, it seemed prudent not to be the game player who officially invited the agency to visit the world of MMOs and gave the feds the opening to tax virtual income. That decision might force game companies, as John Knight had put it, "to start sending out 1099s every time somebody gets a gold coin or a bag of grapes or a shiny emerald" in a game's virtual world.

It would certainly transform the thrill of the online quest into distress for the legions of players who couldn't afford to pay their new taxes, and would likely doom my fellow Frogloks, Vah Shir, and other characters to appalling fates. . . .

Julian Dibbell is the author of *My Tiny Life: Crime and Passion in a Virtual World* and has written about digital technology for *Wired*, *Time*, and *Harper's*, among other publications.

Reprinted with permission of *Legal Affairs*.

OWNERSHIP
VS. TERMS
OF SERVICE

The question of what ownership really means in a virtual environment has come up a few times in the previous pages. Among other things, I quoted the Washington patent attorney Stevan Lieberman on intellectual property rights and copyright protection. He said among other things that creators of things are entitled to copyright protection, and it seems reasonable that this protection would extend to virtual creations, but the creators must file for the copyright in the prescribed time frame to get it.

But what about ownership of an object or land? It's one thing to create something, even virtually, and file for your copyright protection in time and then wait for your application to get processed and see if it's approved. If it's approved, then I would think you can be reasonably assured of protection. But what if you buy a parcel of virtual land? Linden Lab has made it clear, in its terms of service and its public statements, that you have ownership rights in the land. But what if you subsequently violate the Second Life terms of service agreement? Can Linden Lab then take away your land?

A former Second Life resident in the latter part of 2006 filed a complaint in the Chester County (Pennsylvania) Court of Common Pleas to get an answer to that question. After Linden Lab took issue with a procedural matter in a land auction in which the resident was involved, it revoked the resident's account, including the assets (which included fairly extensive land holdings) and Linden dollars he had amassed. To the resident, Linden's ability to cut him off from all his virtual assets suggested that "ownership" in Second Life amounted to something different—and certainly something weaker—than what it means in real life. It's tantamount, he said, to a theme park owner cutting off the assets of a vendor who owns a store within the theme park grounds. Just because the vendor's asset is located in the theme park, does this mean that the theme park can take the assets the vendor owns, at least before the vendor has had the chance to exercise all his legal rights?

Many issues are looked at in comments lawyers have made about the case in media coverage of it, but a question it raises is what ownership means when the assets are in an environment that's subject to a terms of service agreement. If a violation of the terms of service agreement means you lose your assets, than to what extent do you really own those assets? Is losing those assets equivalent to my losing my house in real life if I'm convicted of, say, robbing a bank? Or, can I rob a bank, get caught, tried, convicted, and go to jail, and still retain ownership of my house?

At least one analyst suggested that this case, however it turns out, won't provide a definitive answer to the ownership issue, because ultimately it's about a violation of the terms of service agreement, but given its role as a first attempt to at least raise the ownership issue, I've reproduced the complaint here in its entirety.

CHESTER COUNTY COURT OF COMMON PLEAS
CIVIL COVER SHEET

Do not staple or attach on this side

08 OCT -4 PM 12: 19

OFFICE OF THE
PROTHONOTARY
CHESTER CO. PA.

1. CASE CAPTION: IA. CASE NO.: 06-08711

MARC BRAGG, ESQ. v LINDEN RESEARCH, INC., a corporation, and PHILIP ROSEDALE, an individual

2. PLAINTIFF(s): (Name, address)

MARC BRAGG, ESQ.
230 WEST MARKET STREET
WEST CHESTER, PA 19382

3. PLAINTIFF'S or (circle one)
DEFENDANT'S COUNSEL: (FILING ATTORNEY)
(Name, firm, address, telephone and attorney ID#)

JASON A. ARCHINACO, ESQ. (Plaintiff Counsel)
WHITE AND WILLIAMS, LLP
THE FRICK BUILDING, SUITE 1001
437 GRANT STREET, PITTSBURGH, PA 15219
(412) 566-3520 PA ID 76691

4. DEFENDANT(s): (Name, address)

LINDEN RESEARCH, INC. 1100 SANSOME
STREET, SAN FRANCISCO, CA 94111

PHILIP ROSEDALE, 2717 PACIFIC AVENUE,
SAN FRANCISCO, CA 94115-1129

5. ARE THERE, ANY RELATED CASES?
(see C.C.R.C.P. 200B)
☐ Yes   ☒ No
IF YES, SHOW CASE NOS. AND CAPTIONS:

6. IF THIS IS AN APPEAL FROM A DISTRICT JUSTICE JUDGMENT, WAS APPELLANT ☐ **PLAINTIFF OR**
☐ **DEFENDANT IN THE ORIGINAL ACTION?**

SPECIFIC PERFORMANCE
EQUITABLE RELIEF

7. CASE CODE: 83 **DESCRIPTION: (see reverse side)** _____

8. IS THIS AN ARBITRATION CASE? ☐ Yes ☒ No   YES   JURY TRIAL DEMANDED
(Arbitration Limit is $50,000. See C.C.R.C.P. 1301. 1)

ARBITRATION CASES ONLY
An Arbitration hearing in this matter is scheduled for
at   in the Jury Lounge,
Chester County Court House, West Chester, PA. The parties and their counsel are directed to report to the Juror's Lounge for an arbitration hearing in this matter on the date and time set forth above.

This matter will be heard by a Board of Arbitrators at the time, date and place specified but, if one or more of the parties is not present at the hearing, the matter may be heard at the same time and date before a judge of the court without the absent party or parties. There is no right to a trial *de novo* on appeal from a decision entered by a judge.

NOTICE OF TRIAL LISTING DATE
Pursuant to C.C.R.C.P. 249.3, if this case is not subject to compulsory arbitration it will be presumed ready for trial twelve (12) months from the date of the initiation of the suit and will be placed on the trial list one (1) year from the date the suit was filed unless otherwise ordered by the Court.

To obtain relief from automatic trial listing a party must proceed pursuant to C.C.R.C.P. 249.3(b), request an administrative conference and obtain a court order deferring the placement of the case on the trial list until a later date.

FILE WITH: Prothonotary of Chester County, 2 North High Street, Suite 130, P.O. Box 2748, West Chester, PA 19380-0991

THIS COVER SHEET IS REQUIRED BY C.C.R.P. 1018.1 N AND MUST BE SERVED UPON ALL OTHER PARTIES TO THE ACTION IMMEDIATELY AFTER FILING. SUBMIT ENOUGH COPIES FOR SERVICE

SEE REVERSE SIDE FOR CASE CODES AND DESCRIPTIONS (DETACH PRIOR TO FILLING OUT)
PROTHONOTARY FORM #146.2 REV. 8/2004

**IN THE COURT OF COMMON PLEAS OF
CHESTER COUNTY, PENNSYLVANIA**

MARC BRAGG, Esq., an individual,

        Plaintiff,

      v.

LINDEN RESEARCH, INC., a corporation,
and PHILIP ROSEDALE, an individual,

        Defendants.

CIVIL DIVISION

No.

COMPLAINT IN CIVIL ACTION

Code:

Filed on behalf of Plaintiff, MARC BRAGG,
Esq., an individual,

NOTICE TO PLEAD

TO: Defendants

    You are hereby notified to file a
written response to the enclosed **Complaint**
within twenty (20) days from the date of
service hereof or a judgment may be entered
against you.

By: _____
   Attorney for Plaintiff

Counsel of record for this party:

Jason A. Archinaco, Esq.
PA. I.D. #76691

WHITE AND WILLIAMS LLP
Firm #683
1001 Frick Building
Pittsburgh, PA 15219

(412) 566-3520

JURY TRIAL DEMANDED

DOCS_PIT 35184v.1

IN THE COURT OF COMMON PLEAS OF
CHESTER COUNTY, PENNSYLVANIA

FILED

06 OCT -4 PM 12: 19

OFFICE OF THE
PROTHONOTARY
CHESTER CO. PA.

MARC BRAGG, Esq., an individual,   )   CIVIL DIVISION
)
                    Plaintiff,   )   No.
)
        v.   )
)
LINDEN RESEARCH, INC., a corporation,   )
and PHILIP ROSEDALE, an individual,   )
)
                    Defendants.   )

NOTICE

You have been sued in Court. If you wish to defend, you must enter a written appearance personally or by attorney and file your defenses or objections in writing with this Court. You are warned that if you fail to do so the case may proceed without you and a judgment may be entered against you without further notice for the relief requested by the Plaintiff. You may lose money or property or other rights important to you.

YOU SHOULD TAKE THIS PAPER TO YOUR LAWYER AT ONCE. IF YOU DO NOT HAVE A LAWYER, GO TO OR TELEPHONE THE OFFICE SET FORTH BELOW. THIS OFFICE CAN PROVIDE YOU WITH INFORMATION ABOUT HIRING A LAWYER.

IF YOU CANNOT AFFORD TO HIRE A LAWYER, THIS OFFICE MAY BE ABLE TO PROVIDE YOU WITH INFORMATION ABOUT AGENCIES THA TM AY OFFER LEGAL SERVICES TO ELIGIBLE PERSONS AT A REDUCED FEE OR NO FEE.

Chester County Bar Association
15 West Gay Street, 2nd Floor
P.O. Box 3191
West Chester, PA 19380
610-692-1889

DOCS_PIT 35184v.1

IN THE COURT OF COMMON PLEAS OF
CHESTER COUNTY, PENNSYLVANIA

FILED

MARC BRAGG, Esq., an individual,) CIVIL DIVISION
)
                   Plaintiff,) No.
)
        v.)
)
LINDEN RESEARCH, INC., a corporation,)
and PHILIP ROSEDALE, an individual,)
)
            Defendants.)

PLAINTIFF'S COMPLAINT IN CIVIL ACTION

AND NOW COMES, the Plaintiff, Marc Bragg, Esq., by and through his attorneys, Jason

A. Archinaco, Esq. and the law firm of WHITE AND WILLIAMS, LLP, and avers as follows:

THE PARTIES

1.   Plaintiff, Marc Bragg (hereinafter "Bragg"), is an adult individual resident of the

County of Chester, Commonwealth of Pennsylvania.

2.   Defendant Linden Research, Inc. (hereinafter "Linden"), is a Delaware

corporation, with a primary business address and at all relevant times, providing its services out

of the State of California at 1100 Sansome Street, San Francisco, CA. Linden uses the name

"Linden Labs" on the internet to conduct business.

3.   Defendant, Phillip Rosedale, (hereinafter "Rosedale") is an adult individual and a

resident of the State of California with an address of 2717 Pacific Avenue, San Francisco, CA

94115-1129.

DOCS_PIT 35184v.1

FACTS

BACKGROUND

4.   Linden operates a massively multiplayer role-playing game ("MMORPG") known as "Second Life" and hosted at http://secondlife.com.

5.   To participate in Second Life, a participant must download Linden's client software and install it on the user's computer. A participant may participate for free, or upgrade to a premium membership.

6.   In Second Life, participants from around the world interact together in a huge "virtual" world / environment.

7.   The virtual world / environment contains many of the real world goods and items from cars to homes to slot machines. Linden represents that it promotes the creation and trade of such goods and items by its participants and refers to such items as "virtual property."

8.   Defendants' computer code was designed and intended to act like real world property that requires the payment of U.S. Dollars to buy, own, and sell that property and to allow for the conveyance of title and ownership rights in that property separate and apart from the code itself, and as such, Plaintiff's rights in the virtual property should be regulated and protected like real world property.

9.   Participants in Second Life create characters called "avatars," develop their own unique reputation and/or buy and sell unique software, encoded and scripted "objects," design numerous creative and unique buildings, clothes, equipment, furnishings, etc., run businesses, and purchase uniquely located and described pieces of "virtual land" from the Defendants.

10.   Although referred to as a "game," Second Life is a business operated to generate a profit for Linden and, upon information and belief, Second Life generates a substantial profit for

-2-

Linden and Rosedale. Rosedale has publicly stated that Second Life is not a game but rather is a "platform."

VIRTUAL WORLDS

11.   Linden is not the only company that operates a virtual world for a profit and, indeed, the industry has become saturated with such games ranging from Blizzard's Worlds of Warcraft, to Sony's Everquest and Star Wars Galaxies. However, unlike the industry leaders, Linden is the only MMORPG that represents that its participants retain / obtain ownership rights to the land they purchase from Linden and retain all intellectual property rights for any virtual items or content created by the participant and, indeed, Linden does not even restrict or disclaim such ownership interests in their "Terms of Service" agreement (hereinafter "TOS").

12.   A virtual world is a place one co-inhabits with hundreds of thousands of other people simultaneously. It is persistent and dynamic, in that the world exists independent of any participant's presence (much like the internet does), and in that a participant's actions can permanently shape the world. Even when one is not in the virtual world, the environment continues to exist and changes over time.

13.   Millions of people with Internet connections are now living large portions of their lives, forming friendships with others, building and acquiring virtual property, forming contracts, substantial business relationships and forming social organizations in these virtual worlds.

14.   These millions of individuals are paying substantial sums of money to exist in these virtual worlds; hundreds of millions of dollars flow into the coffers of Sony, Blizzard, and other companies like Linden that provide the servers upon which these virtual worlds reside. Worlds of Warcraft, for example, boasts a subscriber base in excess of 7 million and is believe to be generating revenues in excess of $1 billion a year annually.

-3-

15. There are no courts, no halls of Congress, and no visible mechanisms for civic governance; however, it is foreseeable to the corporate companies that own these virtual worlds, including Linden, that where large amounts of real money flow, legal consequences must follow and, indeed, Linden enforces its legal rights to payments to which it is entitled, and to protecting its business through real world laws.

16. In many respects, these virtual worlds exist similar to theme parks such as Disney World. Thus, although the park itself is an "attraction" in some respects, like Disney World, shops selling merchandise exist and a variety of transactions occur inside the virtual world just like such shops and transactions occur inside Disney World, and independent of entrance to the park itself. Unlike Disney World where Disney chooses to operate many of the shops and control many of the transactions inside of Disney World, nearly every sale of virtual goods and/or virtual "shops" are operated by the third party individual participants of Second Life, as opposed to Linden itself. Moreover, just like the transactions that occur inside Disney World are subject to the laws of the United States of America, so too are the transactions that occur inside and in connection with Second Life.

17. Unlike Disney World, however, Linden has been in the business of selling the land inside the "theme park". Thus, Linden no longer owns the very world they created, instead choosing to sell the world / land to consumers. Rosedale has referred generally to Second Life as a "country."

18. In other respects, Second Life itself is much like Microsoft's Internet Explorer in that it simply gives a participant access to a "world" (like the internet), where the "participant" can enter into a variety of transactions and visit various places. In many respects, Second Life is simply a three-dimensional version of Microsoft's Internet Explorer – and the places one can

-4-

visit using that graphical three-dimensional web browser are simply three dimensional graphical web sites. Rosedale has acknowledged that "Second Life is like the internet but it's 3-D . . . ."

19. Unlike Microsoft's Internet Explorer, however, participants can "see" the other visitors to various "web sites" and locations and choose to interact with them by "chatting" with them.

20. This similarity has lead some commentators to note that Second Life is, in actuality, an operating system like Microsoft Windows and is ultimately designed to compete with Microsoft's Windows. Rosedale has called Second Life a "platform."

VIRTUAL ITEM AND PROPERTY OWNERSHIP

21. Typically, in such virtual worlds, the operators of the worlds claim to not permit the participants to hold any rights to "virtual items" (houses, buildings, cars and other virtual objects) or "virtual land" that exist inside the game world. Both are referred to generally by participants in such worlds as "virtual property."

22. Indeed, several of such companies who have not provided any rights to the participants have threatened lawsuits to prevent the trade and sale of virtual items, land, money and accounts and have attempted to prevent the sale and trade of virtual items, land, money, goods and even the accounts that contain such virtual items, lands, money and goods

23. Generally speaking, most virtual worlds derive their revenue and profit, not from the sale of virtual items, land, money or goods, but rather from monthly subscription fees paid to the operator of the world.

24. The industry standard has generally been to deny that the participant holds any rights in the virtual items, land, money and/or goods that the participant holds in his account. This denial is despite the growing body of legal work that sets forth that, irrespective of such

-5-

company's claims, that participants in such worlds can and do have rights to their virtual property and that any statements or claims to the contrary are unconscionable.

25.   Despite such denials of ownership by participants, the trade of virtual items, land, money and goods is believed, by some estimates, to have approached nearly $1 billion annually and is, in any event, a market and industry in excess of $100 million a year.

26.   Further, despite such a prospering "black market" for virtual items, land, money and goods, because such transactions have been branded as "illegitimate" by the operators of many (if not most) of the virtual worlds, many participants in such virtual worlds have refrained from buying or selling virtual items, land, money and goods despite their rights to do so.

27.   In many respects, a golden opportunity had existed for some time for any virtual world game company that would claim and represent to legitimize the buying and selling of virtual items, land, money and goods by the payment and exchange of U.S. Dollars and that would preserve and protect the participant's intellectual property and ownership rights in any items or goods created inside the game world by the participant.

SECOND LIFE'S PLACE IN THE CROWDED MMORPG MARKET

28.   When Second Life was first "opened" by Linden in 2003, the competition in the industry for participants in virtual worlds was fierce and the industry was dominated by well-known players.

29.   Upon information and belief, Linden had difficulty differentiating itself from other, higher profile games and turning a profit for Linden.

30.   Initially, Linden chose the familiar route of refusing to recognize the participants' rights to the virtual property in-game.

DOCS_PIT 35184v.1

31.   Second Life, unlike other virtual worlds, was devoid of any name recognition, fancy graphics or exciting game-play. As such, Second Life generally languished and trailed its peers in terms of participants.

32.   As such, desperate for a participant base to generate profits, Linden made a calculated business decision to depart from the industry standard of denying that participants had any rights to virtual items, land and/or goods. Linden decided that it could maximize its own profits if it, instead, represented to the participants in its world that their rights to the virtual items, land and goods held in the participants' accounts would be preserved and recognized for the participant and that participants' intellectual property rights are preserved.

33.   Linden announced its new business model at the "State of Play" conference in or about November, 2003 and followed with a press release shortly thereafter.

34.   Linden and Rosedale made oral representations at the "State of Play," and then reduced those representations to writing.

35.   In the November 14, 2003 press release, Linden touted its modifications to Second Life's Terms of Service, stating that "the revised TOS allows subscribers to retain full intellectual property protection for the digital content they create."

36.   In the same press release, Linden, by and through Rosedale, stated: "Until now, any content created by users for persistent state worlds, such as EverQuest or Star Wars Galaxies, has essentially become the property of the company developing and hosting the world," said Rosedale. "We believe our new policy recognizes the fact that persistent world users are making significant contributions to building these worlds and should be able to both own the content they create and share in the value that is created. The preservation of users' property rights is a necessary step toward the emergence of genuinely real online worlds."

-7-

37. Linden's claims to allow Second Life participants to retain their intellectual property rights was even believed by well-known, Stanford University Professor of Law, and Founder of the Stanford Center for Internet and Society, Lawrence Lessig.

38. Indeed, Lessig had such confidence and belief in the representations made by Linden and Rosedale that he permitted himself to be quoted in the November 14, 2003 press release and stated that: "Linden Lab has taken an important step toward recognizing the rights of content generators in Second Life . . . As history has continually proven, when people share in the value they create, greater value is derived for all. Linden Lab is poised for significant growth as a result of this decision."

39. As set forth above, even the well known law professor believed the press release and statements of Linden and noted that Linden was "poised for significant growth" as a result of the decision.

40. Following those representations that were widely regarded as revolutionary to the virtual world industry, Linden's participant base greatly expanded, as predicted by Lessig.

41. Further, in December, 2003, Linden and Rosedale again decided to attempt to increase the participant base of Second Life by representing that participants could own "virtual land" inside of Second Life.

42. The land owned by the participants was taxed by Linden. Indeed, by June 3, 2004, as Rosedale acknowledged to the USA Today, the real estate tax revenue on land sold to the participants exceeded the amount the company was generating in subscriptions.

43. Similarly, in 2004, Rosedale was quoted: "The idea of land ownership and the ease with which you can own land and do something with it…is intoxicating." Rosedale fully

expressed his concept of land ownership by admitting that "land ownership feels important and tangible. It's a real piece of the future."

44.   Thus, by mid-2004, Linden and Rosedale's representations had caused significant dollars to not only be invested in Second Life, through the purchase of virtual land, but also a significant revenue stream generated from the taxation of that virtual land.

45.   Linden and Rosedale continued their publicity campaign regarding ownership rights in Second Life in an effort to continue increasing the participant base and the profits to both Linden and Rosedale.

46.   Defendants published their representations on the Second Life website, including a section called "Own Virtual Land" which discusses "owning land" in Second Life. Defendants also published on the Second Life website a section entitled "IP Rights" which stated that "Linden Lab's Terms of Service agreement recognizes Residents' right to retain full intellectual property protection for the digital content they create in Second Life . . . . This right is enforceable and applicable both in-world and offline . . . You create it, you own it – and it's yours to do with as you please."

47.   On or about June 14, 2005 an interview with Rosedale was published by Guardian Unlimited: Gamesblog. During the course of that interview, Rosedale represented to the world that participants that purchased land in Second Life owned the land.

48.   In response to a question about the integration of Western Capitalism into the Second Life world, Rosedale represented / stated: "We like to think of Second Life as ostensibly as real as a developing nation…The fundamental basis of a successful developing nation is property ownership…**We started selling land free and clear, and we sold the title, and we**

DOCS_PIT 35184v.1

made it extremely clear that we were not the owner of the virtual property." (emphasis added)

49.   As Linden and Rosedale's representations about ownership of land in Second Life continued and as Linden and Rosedale continued to represent that the participants in Second Life retained their intellectual property rights, the participant base for Second Life continued to grow – and generate more money for Linden and Rosedale.

50.   As of September 8, 2005 Defendants representations with regard to virtual land ownership have been so successful that Linden has eliminated subscription fees. In commenting on the elimination of subscription fees in an article posted at CNET news and in disclosing the profit motive of Defendants, Rosedale stated: "We're going to make more [money] because some people who wouldn't have otherwise signed up are going to buy land . . . ."

51.   As of March 28, 2006, the efforts at convincing consumers that they, in fact, would own the land they bought from Defendants, was so successful that a company press release touted that "Second Life has grown to over 165,000 residents with an economy worth over $60mm per year." Linden boasted that "Second Life has enjoyed month over month record growth in subscriber acquisition, its economy and the number of subscribers that are generating profits in US currency."

52.   Further, the March 28, 2006 press release continued Defendants' scheme of associating themselves with well-known and respected figures in an effort to further "legitimize" the representations they were making to consumers at large. Like the prior press release where Defendants associated themselves with Lawrence Lessig, the respected legal scholar, the March, 2006 press release announced that Linden had obtained $11mm in new financing from Globespan Capital Partners, with participation from Jeff Bezos, the founder of Amazon.com.

Linden also noted that other investors, including Mitch Kapor, the founder of Lotus Development Corp., was also involved in their business as an investor. It is believed, and therefore averred, that Defendants have not disclosed to Lessig, Bezos or Kapor that the representations that they make to consumers about land ownership in Second Life are false.

53.   Defendants have aligned themselves in the media with their investors, including Kapor, because as Rosedale states they are interested in the "social good" of technology.

54.   Even recently, Rosedale represented on April 13, 2006 in an interview with PSFK.com, in response to question about whether there was any "gray area" with regard to copyright and intellectual property rights in Second Life, that: "Things are pretty clear – as a user, you own what you create in Second Life." Further, In discussing the importance of land ownership and quoting the concepts set forth in Hernando de Soto's "The Mystery of Capital", Rosedale stated: "[S]uccessful countries always start by making sure that people can freely own, resell, and mortgage the real-estate on which they live. This is a Very Big Idea . . . This was one of the key things that drove our ideas around land ownership and the introduction of IP rights."

55.   Thus, Rosedale continued the façade that Plaintiff and others actually owned the virtual property they purchased from Defendants and, in explaining that Second Life was akin to a country, added further "credibility" to the representations he and Linden were making to consumers at large.

56.   As is more fully set forth at length herein, it was the following month, in May, 2006, that Defendants simply took Plaintiff's virtual land and other virtual items from him without compensation.

57.   Despite Defendants acts that were inconsistent with their public announcements with regard to virtual land ownership and IP right retention, Rosedale and Linden continued with

DOCS_PIT 35184v.1

their public campaign to attract new participants with their promised "utopia" of virtual ownership rights. Approximately two months after stealing Plaintiff's virtual land and property, Rosedale gave a "podcast" interview with After TV on or about July 20, 2006. During that interview, Rosedale continued to reinforce the representations being made. In relevant part Rosedale stated that "everything inside it [Second Life] is made by the people who are there and in fact, the land itself and the space and everything is owned, controlled and built by the people who are there. . . ."

58. Further, when asked by the reporter about how one goes about "owning land" in Second Life, Rosedale replied "You just buy it." Further, he stated "You buy it generally from other users. You can participate in a land auction and buy it from us . . . ."

59. Rosedale was also asked: "So your economic model is selling virtual land; do you have an advertising model?" In response, Rosedale stated, in relevant part: ". . . everyone owns their own stuff, their own property – **there's no way we could just advertise on that property without asking because it isn't ours you know. It belongs to land owners.**" (emphasis added).

60. Rosedale also admitted in the After TV interview that "The majority of our money is made in recurring fees—think of them being like property taxes that you pay when you own land."

61. By July, 2006, the representations of Defendants succeeded in growing the participant base to over 300,000.

62. As set forth previously, the course of representations by Linden and Rosedale resulted in an increased participant base and more profit for each.

63.   It is believed, and therefore averred, that following each substantial press release / interview that the participant base of Second Life spiked and continued to grow.

64.   The announcements and representations of Linden and Rosedale have been very successful for Linden and Rosedale. Indeed, Linden currently boasts it has over 500,000 participants (up from less than 200,000 approximately six months ago) and generates over $50,000,000.00 U.S. per year in real world dollar transactions.

VIRTUAL PROPERTY IN SECOND LIFE

65.   As set forth above and herein, Linden represented that it recognized rights of in-game participants to their virtual items, land, money and goods. Moreover, Linden represented that it recognized the intellectual property rights of the participants in their creations.

66.   The virtual items created by participants as well as the land owned by the participants is retained, preserved and stored by Linden on its servers.

67.   In other words, a participant's account and valuables of Second Life are stored as electromagnetic records on the Linden's servers. Defendants are simply paid for that storage and to hold the land and objects in trust for the owners of the virtual items and property.

68.   The owner of the account is entitled to control the account and valuables' electromagnetic record and may freely sell or transfer it. Although a participant's account and valuables are "virtual," they are valuable property in the real world. The participants can auction them, sell them, license them or transfer them online and through other third independent parties, like eBay.com, slexchange.com, and others.

69.   A participant can sell any code / virtual items they offer; may restrict the code so the purchaser cannot modify it, resell it or transfer it at all; alternatively, participants author code that allows the buyer to resell it that may require the buyer to pay the seller for each such sale.

-13-

DOCS_PIT 35184v.1

70.   Simply put, the system of transferring the virtual items and objects created by a participant mirrors that of the real world in nearly every respect. As set forth previously, similar to a store that exists inside Disney World, participants list and sell their goods and virtual items for sale or trade.

71.   A participant's accounts and valuables are the same as the property in the real world.

72.   A participant's interests in these virtual items, objects and properties persist regardless of the system currently connected to it, separate from the intellectual property that exists in Defendants' underlying code, much similar to a document or book simply created with a program such as Microsoft Word. Indeed, some commentators have noted that Second Life is, in essence, simply an "operating system" similar to Microsoft Windows.

73.   A participant can invite people into his virtual property, hold meetings in it, invest in it, and sell it to other people who might want to do the same independent of and regardless of the intellectual property that exists in Defendants' code.

74.   Accordingly, Plaintiff's virtual property rights are divisible and severable from the rights of other participants in the game and the owner of the server upon which Defendants' code resides.

75.   These virtual properties, both the virtual land and the virtual objects, have value in real U.S. Dollars across the globe measuring in the billions of dollars and millions of participants.

76.   Defendants intended their code and their public statements regarding ownership and use rights of the land and objects to materially induce Plaintiff as well as thousands of other

-14-

participants to invest real U.S. Dollars in purchasing land, and buying and selling the objects described above and have actively encouraged participants to do so.

77.   Because of Defendants' transfer of title and ownership interests to Plaintiff in their virtual assets, and Defendant's creation of a market economy in which Plaintiff's property interests may be sold for real cash value, expectations that these virtual assets constitute property are entirely foreseeable, in addition to the representations made by Linden and Rosedale specifically providing for such property rights and the preservation of the same.

78.   Along with Defendants' promise of the transfer of title to Plaintiff of the title to their land and the ownership rights to their copyright and intellectual property creations, Defendants' virtual world possesses all of the real world features of exclusive ownership; persistence of rights, transfer under conditions of agreement and duress, free alienability of title, and a currency system to support trade in these property-based assets, including the buying and selling of these assets with U.S. currency. Private property is the default in Defendants' service, providing its customers with a bundle of rights, including the fundamental rights to use, exclude and transfer property interests.

VIRTUAL PROPERTY IN SECOND LIFE – PROPERTY OWNERSHIP

79.   For a participant to purchase and own land in Second Life, the participant must upgrade to a premium membership and pay a monthly "tier," or tax which varies in amount depending on the amount of land the participant owns.

80.   A participant may then, in his unbridled discretion and control, split the land into varying sizes and parcels, resell it to other participants and convey title, retain it, build upon it, restrict what can be built upon it, change the shape of the land, i.e. "terraform" it, rent it, lease it, and / or exclude all participants, or just some participants from trespassing upon it. While

-15-

DOCS_PIT 35184v.1

Linden continues to create "new" land, once land is created and/or sold to a participant, it continues to exist and is not "deleted" or otherwise destroyed. It is unique, just like real land.

81. To obtain premier accounts, participants are required to provide Defendants with private and confidential information including a credit card number and associated information so it can be charged, or a PayPal account to debit. Defendants retain participants' personal information on their servers.

82. Participants access their personal account information, purchase "lindens" (the in-game money), buy and sell lindens for U.S. currency, pay for land, and monitor their accounts via the Internet. A currency exchange is maintained that sets, just like any other currency exchange, the exchange rate between "lindens" and U.S. currency. Third parties also provide for additional currency exchanges between "lindens" and U.S. currency, including ebay.com.

83. Defendants' website expressly states that a participant may cancel an account at any time and leads one to believe that upon canceling, their private account information, such as their credit card information or PayPal account information, will be destroyed and no longer used or retained or made available to the public.

MARC BRAGG IS INDUCED INTO "PARTICIPATING" IN THE SECOND LIFE WORLD

84. Plaintiff is an individual who signed up and paid Defendants to participate in Second Life in or about November / December 2005.

85. Having had prior interest in developing real estate, Bragg was interested in developing the real estate in Second Life upon learning that Defendants had represented that title to the land and all associated ownership rights would pass to the buyer of that land and did so for primarily personal, family and/or household purposes.

DOCS_PIT 35184v.1

86.   Plaintiff was induced into "investing" in and purchasing virtual property from Linden and Rosedale by the representations made by Linden and Rosedale in press releases, interviews and through the Second Life website.

87.   Plaintiff believed the representations made by Linden and Rosedale and justifiably relied upon them. Indeed, there was nothing to make Plaintiff suspect that the representations being made by Linden and Rosedale were false.

88.   By promising Plaintiff that he would receive and retain all right, title, interest, copyright and intellectual property rights to the land, objects and virtual property Plaintiff purchased and/or created in Second Life, Defendants intended to and did in fact deceptively induce Plaintiff to invest thousands in U.S. Dollars via the wires and mails crossing state lines.

89.   Indeed, over the course of his participation in the game, Plaintiff acquired a significant amount of virtual property from Defendants, or others in-game, as set forth and more fully described in Exhibit "1" attached hereto.

90.   Further, Plaintiff acquired a number of virtual items from independent third parties.

SECOND LIFE'S AUCTION OF LAND

91.   Defendants generally sell their lands via auctions hosted on Defendants' website.

92.   On their website, Defendants identify various ways to discover which pieces of virtual land, or "sims," are being auctioned; (1) by reviewing the list posted on the secondlife.com website to see land currently on the auction block; and (2) by looking in-game at the land that has been set as a blue square by Defendants.

93.   Defendants used the same color blue for their "sims" to identify three different states of that land:

-17-

a.   Land that was currently on the auction block;

b.   Land that was intended to be auctioned once a participant initiated the auction;

c.   Land that was not on the auction block and where the auction could not be initiated by a participant.

94.   Defendants' FAQ on auctions advised a participant that, in order to find land intended to be auctioned or on the auction block, to go in-game to the Map provided by Defendants showing the squares set in blue by Defendants to determine which "sims" are to be auctioned.

95.   Any participant that would go in-game to those blue squares could obtain data associated with that particular blue square via the tools provided by Defendants. That data included the land size, name of the "sim", and a unique auction ID (which is the number associated in the auctions for that particular "sim").

96.   If a participant wanted to bid on an auction, Defendants provided unique auction pages for each piece of land being auctioned which allowed the participant to enter the amount they intended to bid, confirm the bid, advising the participant that any bid won constituted a "legal and binding contract," and then once bid, posting the amount bid on that auction page for anyone to review and bid against.

97.   A participant was allowed to either go to the auctions listed by Defendants on their ongoing auction page and bid there, or to enter the unique auction ID number in the URL provided by Defendants for auctions, and by so doing, initiate an auction for only those blue squares set by Defendants allowing the initiation to occur.

-18-

98.   Moreover, a participant could go to Google.com and conduct a search by entering the query "second life auctions [sim name or id number]" and Google would return a link to the various auctions; both those that were ongoing having been initiated by Defendants and those where participants could initiate the auction.

99.   In all cases, the auction would then run for 48 or 72 hours at which time anyone else who was aware of the auction and wanted to bid on the land was free to do so.

100.   Once auctions were won, participants were charged for the purchase of the land at the final bid price via their credit cards and/or PayPal accounts, or by deducting the U.S. currency in their accounts then held in trust by Defendants for such purposes.

101.   Moreover, once the auction closed, the name of the "sim," winning participant's name, and final amount bid were displayed on the secondlife.com website.

102.   At no point prior to, during or following the sale of the virtual property via the auctions, did Defendants advise Plaintiff, or any participant for that matter, that their public representations that Plaintiff would own all right, title and interest in such land were false or otherwise misleading. Indeed, Defendants continued with their ruse to cause Plaintiff to believe that the virtual land sold to Plaintiff by Defendants and all right, title and interest to such land had been transferred or otherwise provided to Plaintiff.

103.   Defendant's auctions, being held in California, are controlled by California Civil Code §1812.600 et seq., the statute relating to auctions held in California.

104.   Each and every virtual land purchase, independently, was a valid and enforceable contract for which Plaintiff paid valuable consideration either from Defendants or from third-parties in-game.

105.   Plaintiff deposited real world money with Linden to obtain the land.

DOCS_PIT 35184v.1

106. After upgrading to a premium account, Plaintiff paid real world money as "tax" on that land.

107. Plaintiff trusted and believed that the money he deposited with Linden, as well as the money he invested in the virtual property, could not and would not be converted or stolen by the Defendants. Further, Plaintiff trusted and believed that Linden's representations that Plaintiff would retain all of his intellectual property rights were true and that Defendants would not interfere in the use and/or exercise of those rights.

"[Y]OU CAN'T FOR EXAMPLE JUST TAKE SOMEONE ELSE'S PROPERTY IN SECOND LIFE", (PHILIP ROSEDALE, JULY 20, 2006), i.e. LINDEN STEALS BRAGG'S PROPERTY

108. In or about April, 2006, Bragg had significantly grown his real estate holdings as well as his own virtual goods, items and content that he had created and offered for sale. Indeed, not only had Bragg purchased numerous parcels of land from Defendants, but he had also created content such as "fireworks" that Plaintiff offered for sale and did sell to other participants. Plaintiff had also acquired numerous other virtual items from third-parties, independent of Defendants.

109. Bragg learned through other participants, messages posted by Defendants' agents in Defendants' forums on Defendants' website, and by Defendants' agents in forums hosted by Linden Labs that there was more than one way to purchase land from Defendants via Defendants' auctions.

110. Until April, 2006, Bragg had acquired all land he purchased via ongoing auction or other sellers within Second Life.

111. On or about April 30, 2006, Bragg bid on and subsequently won the bid on a piece of virtual land named "Taessot." Bragg paid Defendants $300.00 in U.S. currency for that land, which amount Defendants accepted per the terms of their "legally binding contract" and

DOCS_PIT 35184v.1

-20-

transferred title to Bragg. The purchase of the land was memorialized on Defendants' closed auction list reflecting the price paid.

112. On or about May 2, 2006 or May 3, 2006, however, Bragg received an e-mail from "Jack Linden," a Linden agent, employee and/or servant, advising Bragg that the Taessot land had been purchased using an "exploit" in the system, and accordingly, the land had been taken away from Bragg and further, that Bragg would receive his $300.00 U.S. currency refunded to him.

113. The statements of the Linden agent were a lie, however. While Defendants did remove Bragg's name from the title to the Taessot land, they failed and refused to return Bragg's $300 to him that they had agreed to refund.

114. Even worse and deceptive, Linden "froze" Bragg's account preventing him from accessing the account to use, cancel or modify it. In essence, Linden prevented Bragg from access any of his items, land or goods to which he had all rights, title and interest. Moreover, despite preventing Bragg access to his items, land and goods, Linden continued to charge Bragg a "tax" on the land he owned and, also, refused to release Bragg's credit card information.

115. In the ultimate act of deception and fraud, Linden, without any right to do so or any consent from Bragg, removed Bragg's name from all other land owned by Bragg as described in Exhibit "1." Moreover, Linden proceeded to convert the title and all associated value away from Bragg without notice, process of any kind, reimbursement, or consideration of any kind.

116. Such actions were taken despite Rosedale's specific admission and statement on July 20, 2006 that **"you can't for example just take someone else's property in Second Life."** (emphasis added). Moreover, Rosedale's comment was made in the context of him referring to

DOCS_PIT 35184v.1

such an act as a **crime**. Rosedale's statements are an admission against he and Linden that Defendants acts were improper and, in fact, a crime.

117. The land that Bragg owned was taken from him but not "deleted" from the game world. Indeed, had Linden done so, it would have undermined their own plan to enrich themselves at the expense of Plaintiff. See, Exhibit "2," map of Second Life world, attached hereto.

118. In so wrongfully taking Bragg's land, Defendants also removed, retained, and/or converted all other personal property and objects then owned by Bragg in-game, all of which Bragg had purchased with U.S. currency, and all of which, including the land, had real value and could have been sold to multiple ready, willing and able buyers. Bragg was never offered the opportunity to do so. Defendants also interfered and prevented Plaintiff from exploiting his rights to sell and/or otherwise trade his "fireworks" and other content created by him and, in which, he retained all intellectual property rights.

119. Defendants took, retained and converted Bragg's virtual property, without just cause, excuse or notice of any kind, including his virtual land, buildings, businesses, code scripted objects, and linden dollars all of which had been purchased with real world U.S. dollars as a result of Defendants' fraudulent representations.

120. Moreover, Bragg had a significant amount of U.S. currency in his account, approximately $2000. Linden simply took the money, along with all of Bragg's other possessions. Despite approximately 50 attempts to withdraw his money from the account, Linden blocked those transactions and prevented Bragg from transferring his money.

121. With regard to the land owned by Bragg and wrongfully confiscated and taken by Linden, Defendants listed the property at auction and sold it to the highest bidder.

DOCS_PIT 35184v.1

122.   In the ultimate act of fraudulent bravado, Defendants kept the proceeds of the auctions of Bragg's land for themselves and provided none of the money to Bragg. In essence, Defendants had doubled their own profits by charging twice for the same land – and unjustly enriching themselves at the expense of an unsuspecting Bragg who had been defrauded.

123.   Thus, not only did Defendants "eject" Bragg from their "Disney World," but before doing so, they confiscated all the goods he had purchased at the stores, refused to refund his money for the purchases, re-listed the purchased goods for re-sale, resold the goods to third parties, did not provide the proceeds to Bragg (keeping it for themselves) and – to top it off – simply took his other possessions as well as his wallet (with all his U.S. currency in it) that Bragg had, evidently, made the serious mistake of bringing into the "park" with him.

124.   Defendants' conduct as described is part of a continuing and systematic plan and scheme using the national wires and mails intended to and in fact defrauding Plaintiff and other similarly situated consumers out of thousands of dollars by promising to preserve and/or otherwise provide rights that the Defendants do not provide and, indeed, lie about to potential participants.

125.   The utopia of Second Life and the promise by Defendants to potential participants that they will retain all rights, title and interest in the virtual land, property and goods was a lie. Apparently, Defendants never intended to perform according to their promises and representations.

SECOND LIFE'S ATTEMPTED FINE PRINT, AKA THE TERMS OF SERVICE AGREEMENT ("TOS")

126.   Defendants provide what is known as a Terms of Service Agreement ("TOS"). Although referred to as a TOS, the reality is that the "agreement" is nothing more than a contract

-23-

of adhesion. Like many participants, Bragg never read the TOS although he was forced to click the "accept" button to gain access to his virtual property, land and items.

127.   Defendants' TOS is very similar, in essence, to the fine print on the back of a ticket checking your automobile with a valet or, similarly, entrance to a theme park.

128.   Like the unconscionable terms contained with such contracts of adhesion that provide the potential participant with absolutely no negotiating leverage, the Linden TOS is similarly drafted in such an unconscionable, heavy handed way. Moreover, the TOS is consistently changed and, despite the fact a participant may "join" while one TOS is in "effect" and already "invested" thousands of dollars based on one TOS, the participant is forced to "accept" any revised TOS to gain access to his virtual property, land and items. Thus, Linden simply unilaterally imposes any contract terms on the participant without regard to whether the participant signed up under a different TOS and without consideration.

129.   Further, like such fine print on access to a theme park, the TOS is naturally limited and cannot possibly apply to any valid transaction that occurs within the theme park itself. Thus, similar to the fact shops operate inside of Disney World (selling all types of goods and items), many operated by Disney itself, and others operated by third parties, the laws of the United States of America do not cease to exist inside of a theme park like Disney World, irrespective of any fine print on the back of a ticket providing access to Disney World. Indeed, such fine print could not possibly operate to suspend the laws of the United States inside of Disney World, nor the transactions that occur inside its "walls." Equally, no fine print provided by Defendants could possibly operate to suspend the laws of the United States inside of Second Life.

-24-

DOCS_PIT 35184v.1

130.   Indeed, any attempt to claim that the TOS effectively operates, in any way, to suspend the laws of the United States, is simply unconscionable and absurd.

131.   While Defendants provide a TOS, it did not state or provide any term or condition such that Defendants may retain and/or convert Bragg's money, or that Plaintiff ever waived the right to, retain and remove, Plaintiff's property interests or his U.S. currency on deposit held in trust with Defendants.   Moreover, the TOS does not address deleting land and, in fact, the land existing in Second Life is never deleted, instead persisting with a name, size and location, all the things that make "real property" unique.

132.   Indeed, any such terms would be utterly inconsistent with the repeated representations made by Defendants in the media and press.

133.   To the extent that Defendants seek to interpret their own TOS inconsistently with the representations made by them to the world in the media and press or that Defendants may withhold, retain, and/or convert Plaintiff's property interests or Plaintiff's U.S. currency on deposit in trust with Defendants in any way, shape or form, such terms and/or conditions are unconscionable and should otherwise be deemed void as against public policy and not enforceable.

134.   Further, Defendants' TOS provides no clear or reasonable notice to Plaintiff that Defendants may at any time, without notice, and/or without identifying a violation of Defendants' TOS, or in fact there being a violation of Defendants' TOS, withhold, retain, and/or convert all property interests and U.S. Currency belonging to the Plaintiff. Even if the TOS did contain any such terms, they would be unconscionable and unenforceable.

135.   The TOS provides, in relevant part, the following misleading assertions:

DOCS_PIT 35184v.1

a.   "The Websites and Linden Software collectively constitute the "Service" as used in this Agreement"; however, the TOS does not claim that the software created by participants is controlled by the TOS (Section 1.1);

b.   in Section 1.2, that "Linden Lab is a service provider, which means.... that Linden Lab does not control various aspects of the service" leading Plaintiff to believe that he, consistent with Defendants' public representations regarding ownership rights, instead controlled those aspects of his investments;

c.   in Section 1.3, that "Linden Lab and other parties have rights in their respective content, which you agree to respect" leading Plaintiff to believe that he had full ownership and title rights in his content, and that Defendants would respect and preserve same to the best of their ability;

d.   in Section 1.3, that "Linden Lab and other Content Providers [which includes Plaintiff] have rights in their respective Content under copyright and *other applicable laws* and treaty provisions, and that except as described in this Agreement, such rights are not licensed or otherwise transferred by mere use of the Service[]" leading Plaintiff to believe that by investing thousands of dollars in U.S. currency constitutes something substantially more than "mere use" of the Service and that investment was not subject to conversion, fraudulent or otherwise, by Defendants;

e.   in Section 1.4, establishing a "currency" (Linden Dollar) and granting a limited license to same, but not otherwise limiting or restricting Plaintiff's rights to withdraw U.S. currency in their respective accounts, and not clearly explaining that the limited license right could be revoked or modified as a single or group of users, instead suggesting that

Defendants' right to modify the limited license right it granted would be applied to all participants, and not selectively modified for one or more;

      f.   in Section 1.5, explaining that the use of the words "buy" and "sell" on their website is used to indicate the transfer of the limited license right described in Section 1.4, and stating that Defendants may deny any sell order individually "for any reason," which terms are unconscionable and contrary to, but not in any way suggesting that, the U.S. currency in Plaintiff's account was subject to the above arbitrary standard;

      g.   further, in Section 1.5, the arbitrary standard of "for any reason" being unconscionable, it should be deemed void and of no force or effect;

      h.   in Section 1.7, providing that participants agree to the posted pricing and billing policies on the Websites, which in relevant part under the common law reciprocal rights pursuant to contract law in California, requires Defendants then to abide by its posted pricing and billing policies, which would require Defendants to honor all auctions that were closed and paid for and all title transfers in connection with them;

      i.   in Section 2.5, providing that any participant may cancel an account at any time and in not stating or otherwise suggestion that any such cancellation would forfeit any and/or all U.S. currency placed and/or transferred into Plaintiff's account;

      j.   in Section 2.6, providing that Defendants may "suspend or terminate your account any time, without refund or obligation," but not otherwise providing that the assets and ownership interests conveyed by Defendants and/or third parties would be retained by Defendants, or otherwise unrecoverable. Moreover, to the extent that Defendants attempt to interpret Section 2.6 inconsistently with their public statements and representations, they should be estopped from doing so and any interpretation inconsistent with their public representations is

-27-

DOCS_PIT 35184v.1

unconscionable and/or any interpretation that Section 2.6 is tantamount to any "right" of Defendants to convert the property and/or currency of Plaintiff, such an interpretation is unconscionable and unenforceable as a matter of law;

      k.   in Section 3.1, providing that participants have a nonexclusive, limited, revocable license which is not subject to revocation for so long as the participant is in compliance with the TOS;

      l.   in Sections 3.2 and 3.3, granting Defendants the irrevocable rights to delete all data stored on Defendants' servers, and granting ownership of the "account" only in Defendants, but not otherwise granting Defendants the right to convert Plaintiff's U.S. currency held in trust by Defendants, or the title to the virtual property conveyed to Plaintiff to the extent the data representing that property has not been deleted or, further, the right to interfere with the intellectual property rights of the participant. Moreover, to the extent that Defendants attempt to interpret Section 3.2 or 3.3 inconsistently with their public statements and representations, they should be estopped from doing so and any interpretation inconsistent with their public representations is unconscionable and/or any interpretation that Sections 3.2 and 3.3 is tantamount to any "right" of Defendants to convert the property and/or currency of Plaintiff, such an interpretation is unconscionable and unenforceable as a matter of law

      m.   in Section 4.1, defining community standards, but not stating any standard by which Plaintiff's actions while a participant could be reasonably deemed to have violated any of the stated community standards;

      n.   in Section 5, et seq., providing various releases in favor of Defendants, many of which are unconscionable, and/or require mutuality, and none of which release Defendants from any claim for conversion of the U.S. currency held in trust by Defendants in favor of Plaintiff, or release Defendants for conversion of assets and data belonging to Plaintiff that have not been deleted (i.e., the land purchased by Plaintiff), or release Defendants for damages caused by interfering with prospective economic advantage or economic relations between participants, or release Defendants for intentionally destroying Plaintiff's data with an intent to harm and without any proper purpose;

    .   o.   in Section 5.4, acknowledging that certain limitations and terms stated in the TOS may not be enforceable in various jurisdictions.

136.   Defendants' representations regarding the transfer of full and alienable title to participants upon the purchase of land, and the transfer of ownership rights consequent to participants' copyright and trademark interests, and Plaintiff's consideration given in light of those statements, are material modifications to the TOS to the extent those statements by Defendants are contrary to the written terms of the TOS.

137.   Further, Defendants did not state in their TOS that they had the unfettered right to take back the title to any of the land they sold nor did Defendants provide any process for the recovery of title from their participants. Further, the TOS does not state that Defendants have the unfettered right to obstruct or otherwise impede a participants use of his intellectual property rights or that the TOS governs or acts to otherwise interfere with transactions between third parties.

138.   In essence, despite Defendants' public statements regarding land ownership and the retention of intellectual property rights, representations that they used and are using to build their participant base, Defendants simply depart from those public statements at their own whim and for their own profits.

-29-

DOCS_PIT 35184v.1

COUNT I: VIOLATION OF THE PENNSYLVANIA UNFAIR TRADE PRACTICES AND CONSUMER PROTECTION LAW (73 P.S. § 201-1, et. seq.)

139.   Plaintiff hereby incorporates by reference Paragraphs 1 through 138, as more fully set forth above.

140.   Plaintiff acquired virtual land, property and items from Defendants primarily for personal, family and/or household purposes.

141.   Defendants knowingly and actively represented that title to land (and virtual items) purchased in Second Life and all associated ownership rights would pass to the buyer Plaintiff.

142.   Defendants also knowingly and actively represented that participants in Second Life would retain all of their intellectual property rights.

143.   The representations of Defendants were false as to the virtual land, property, items and intellectual property rights and violated, at a minimum, 73 P.S. § 201-2 (4): (v), (ix) and (xxi).

144.   Further, Defendants never explicitly stated that depositing U.S. currency with Defendants in an account was, in truth, a forfeiture of such real world money. Indeed, every statement made by Defendants gave the appearance, impression and deceptively caused Plaintiff to believe that his real world U.S. currency was actually his own money, and not simply being taken, without his knowledge, by the Defendants for their own unlawful and unjust reasons.

145.   Defendants knowingly and actively concealed their misrepresentations and did not specifically state or otherwise disclose their misrepresentations in their TOS or otherwise as, to do so, would have destroyed the entire purpose of their scheme, unfair methods of competition and/or deceptive acts or practices.

146.   The misrepresentations made by Defendants were material to the transactions at issue and constitute unfair methods of competition and unfair or deceptive acts or practices in violation of 73 P.S. § 201-1, et. seq. and more specifically 73 P.S. § 201-2.

147.   At all times relevant hereto, it was the intent of Defendants to deceive, defraud and induce reliance upon the material misrepresentations. Indeed, the primary purpose of the false statements was to increase the participant base for Second Life under the false pretense that participants in Second Life would acquire rights, title and interests to virtual land, property and items and retain their intellectual property rights, unlike other MMORPG that claim that the participants surrender or fail to possess such rights.

148.   Defendants' statements to the media purporting to give exclusive ownership rights to Plaintiff and other Second Life participants are evidence of their intent to deceive, defraud and/or induce reliance by the Plaintiff to purchase the land and otherwise invest valuable time and consideration in Second Life.

149.   Plaintiff justifiably relied upon the material misrepresentations made by Defendants and purchased the virtual land in question, using U.S. currency, under the belief that title was transferred to him by Defendants and that he would retain all his intellectual property rights.

150.   Had Plaintiff known that the Defendants were making completely false assertions of ownership rights and retention of intellectual property rights and simply a ruse to generate a larger participant base, he would never have purchased the virtual land, property or items or otherwise invested his real world time or U.S. currency in Second Life or with Defendants.

DOCS_PIT 35184v.1

151. Indeed, Defendants knew that no one would invest their time or money with them or in Second Life without the misrepresentations of ownership and retention of intellectual property rights, which is the precise reason they made such false representations.

152. Further, had Plaintiff known that Defendants would, at their whim, repossess and subsequently resell the land in question and keep all the proceeds for themselves to enrich themselves, Plaintiff would never have purchased the land for real world U.S. currency.

153. Had Plaintiff known that Defendants would, at their whim, simply take his real world U.S. currency and keep it for themselves, he would never have entrusted his real world U.S. currency with Defendants and placed such money in any account with Defendants.

154. Defendants acts cause them to be liable pursuant to 73 P.S. § 201-9.2 and Plaintiff is entitled to actual damages or one hundred dollars ($100), whichever is greater, and may be provided such other relief as is deemed necessary and proper, including treble damages and attorneys fees.

155. As a result of the fraudulent and deceptive conduct engaged in by the Defendants, Plaintiff sustained real world damages and was harmed in an amount to be determined at trial.

156. Further, injunctive relief and/or specific performance should be ordered against Defendants as the virtual property owned by Plaintiff was and remains unique and no adequate remedy at law exists with regard to depriving Plaintiff of the use and benefit of his virtual land.

157. Additionally, Defendants have admitted that they have sold title to the virtual land to third parties / participants. As such, Defendants should be enjoined from preventing Plaintiff and/or any other customers from accessing virtual land that is not owned by Defendants that has, instead been sold by Defendants.

158. The Court should further declare that, having sold the virtual land, Defendants no longer have any ownership interest in such land or in those portions of the Second Life world that Defendants sold to third parties, including Plaintiff, other than the express responsibility of Defendants to maintain and/or not take such other acts to preclude or prevent participants from enjoying and utilizing their own virtual land.

159. The Court should also declare that Defendants have no rights to interfere with access to the virtual land owned by Plaintiff and, as such, should require access to such land and, to the extent that Defendants claim otherwise, create an easement to permit such access.

WHEREFORE, Plaintiff Marc Bragg prays this Honorable Court enter judgment for Plaintiff and against Defendants Linden Research, Inc. and Philip Rosedale, for actual, treble and punitive damages, for Defendants' violation in an amount that the Court determines is proper and just, including attorney's fees and costs. Further, Plaintiff requests that the Court issue such additional relief as it deems necessary or proper, including injunctive and declaratory relief that Plaintiff is the rightful owner of the virtual land, property and items that were in his account and has all rights to exploit, transfer and/or otherwise use his intellectual property rights as set forth herein and above.

JURY TRIAL DEMANDED

COUNT II: VIOLATION OF THE CALIFORNIA UNFAIR AND DECEPTIVE PRACTICES ACT (Cal. Bus. & Prof. Code § 17200)

160. Plaintiff hereby incorporates by reference Paragraphs 1 through 159 as more fully set forth above.

161. Defendants knowingly and actively misrepresented to Plaintiff and public as a whole that all right, title and interest to the virtual land and all associated ownership rights would pass to buyers and that Plaintiff would retain his intellectual property rights.

-33-

DOCS_PIT 35184v.1

162.   These misrepresentations were material to the transaction as it involved the development of real estate in Second Life in which Defendants represented that all right, title and ownership rights were to be conferred to buyers and that all intellectual property rights were retained by the participants and/or otherwise preserved.

163.   At all times relevant hereto, it was the intent of Defendants to deceive, defraud and induce reliance of both Plaintiff and public as a whole upon the material misrepresentations.

164.   Such misrepresentations are violations of Cal Civ. Code § 1711 that provides: "One who practices a deceit with intent to defraud the public, or a particular class of persons, is deemed to have intended to defraud every individual in that class, who is actually misled by the deceit."

165.   Plaintiff justifiably relied upon the material misrepresentations made by Defendants and purchased the virtual land in question under the belief that title was transferred to him by Defendants.

166.   Further, Plaintiff justifiably relied upon the material misrepresentations with regard to the preservation and retention of his intellectual property rights.

167.   Had Plaintiff known that Defendants misrepresented ownership rights in order to induce Plaintiff to purchase virtual land, Plaintiff would have never purchased the virtual land and/or otherwise invested his U.S. currency and/or time in Second Life and with Defendants.

168.   Moreover, had Plaintiff known that Defendants, after their misrepresentations, would repossess and subsequently resell the virtual land and interfere and/or destroy his intellectual property rights, Plaintiff would never have purchased the virtual land in the first place nor provided his U.S. currency to Defendants.

169.   The misrepresentations of Defendants as set forth above violated Cal. Civil Code § 1750, and 1770 (a) (7), (9), (16) and (19).

170.   As a result of the fraudulent and deceptive conduct engaged in by the Defendants, Plaintiff sustained damages and was harmed in an amount to be determined at trial.

WHEREFORE, Plaintiff Marc Bragg prays this Honorable Court enter judgment for Plaintiff and against Defendants Linden Research, Inc. and Philip Rosedale, for actual, treble and punitive damages, for Defendants' violation in an amount that the Court determines is proper and just, including attorney's fees and costs.

JURY TRIAL DEMANDED

COUNT III: VIOLATION OF THE CALIFORNIA CONSUMER LEGAL REMEDIES ACT, Ca. Civ. Code § 1750, et. seq.

171.   Plaintiff hereby incorporates by reference Paragraphs 1 through 170, as more fully set forth above.

172.   As set forth above and herein, the acts, statements and material omissions of Defendants constitute violations of the California Consumer Legal Remedies Act, codified at Ca. Civ. Code § 1750, et. seq.

173.   Plaintiff repeatedly placed Defendants upon notice of their violations of his rights that were, in fact, violations of Ca. Civ. Code § 1750, et. seq., including Cal. Civil Code § 1770 (a) (7), (9), (16) and (19).

174.   Plaintiff repeatedly demanded that Defendants correct their violation of Cal. Civil Code § 1770 (a) (7), (9), (16) and (19).

175.   Defendants refused to provide any remedy or correction of their violations.

176.   Accordingly, as a result of Defendants violation of such statute, Plaintiff is entitled to:

DOCS_PIT 35184v.1

a.   Actual damages;

b.   An order enjoining such methods, acts, or practices;

c.   Restitution of property;

d.   Punitive damages; and

e.   Any other relief that the court deems proper.

177.   Plaintiff is further entitled to court costs and attorneys fees due to Defendants' violation of such statute.

WHEREFORE, Plaintiff Marc Bragg prays this Honorable Court enter judgment for Plaintiff and against Defendants Linden Research, Inc. and Philip Rosedale, for actual and punitive damages, for Defendants' violation in an amount that the Court determines is proper and just, including attorney's fees and costs. Further, Plaintiff requests that the Court issue such additional relief as it deems necessary or proper, including injunctive and declaratory relief that Plaintiff is the rightful owner of the virtual land, property and items that were in his account and has all rights to exploit, transfer and/or otherwise use his intellectual property rights.

JURY TRIAL DEMANDED

COUNT IV: FRAUD AND/OR FRAUD IN THE INDUCEMENT

178.   Plaintiff hereby incorporates by reference Paragraphs 1 through 177, as more fully set forth above.

179.   As set forth above and herein, Defendants made:

a.   False representations;

b.   Material to the transaction at hand;

c.   Made falsely and with knowledge of their falsity and/or recklessness as to whether the statements were true and/or false;

DOCS_PIT 35184v.1

-36-

      d.   With the intent of misleading Plaintiff into relying upon the misrepresentations;

      e.   That Plaintiff justifiably relied upon; and

      f.   That caused and/or proximately caused Plaintiff damages and/or injuries.

    180.   As a result of the fraudulent and deceptive conduct engaged in by the Defendants, Plaintiff sustained damages and was harmed in an amount to be determined at trial.

    181.   Plaintiff should be awarded punitive damages because of the egregiousness of the false statements made by Defendants designed to unjustly enrich Defendants at the expense of Plaintiff and others and to reap unjustifiable profits for the Defendants.

    WHEREFORE, Plaintiff Marc Bragg prays this Honorable Court enter judgment for Plaintiff and against Defendants Linden Research, Inc. and Philip Rosedale, for actual and punitive damages, for Defendants' fraud / fraud in the inducement in an amount that the Court determines is proper and just, including attorney's fees and costs.

JURY TRIAL DEMANDED

COUNT V: VIOLATION OF CALIFORNIA CIVIL CODE § 1812.600, et. seq.

    182.   Plaintiff hereby incorporates by reference Paragraphs 1 through 181, as more fully set forth above.

    183.   California Civil Code §1812.600, et. seq., governs auction transactions in or originating from the State of California.

    184.   The sale of the virtual land, as set forth more fully at length herein and above, occurred via and qualifies as an auction pursuant to Cal. Civ. Code §1812.601(b).

    185.   Defendant, Linden, is an "auction company" as that term is defined in Cal. Civ Code §1812.601(c).

-37-

186.   Further, Defendant, Linden, is an auctioneer as that term is defined in Cal. Civ. Code. §1812.601(d).

187.   The virtual property sold by Defendant, Linden, qualifies as a good under Cal. Civ. Code §1812.601(g).

188.   Cal. Civ. Code §1812.600, et. seq., cannot be waived and any attempts waive such code sections are contrary to public policy, void and unenforceable pursuant to Cal. Civ. Code §1812.609.

189.   Upon information and belief, Plaintiff alleges that Defendants have not provided a bond to the California Secretary of State, did not post or distribute the terms, conditions, restrictions, and procedures for the goods sold at their auctions, and upon re-auctioning Plaintiff's land as described below, did not provide Plaintiff with either the information required to be provided and associated with those subsequent auction transactions, or the proceeds thereof, all in violation of various provisions of the above statute including Cal. Civ. Code §§ 1812.600(a)-(c), 1812.607(a), (c), (g), (i), (j), (k), (l), and (m); 1812.608(a), (c), (d), (f), (g), (i), (j) and (k).

190.   Defendant, Linden, also violated Cal. Civ. Code § 1812.605 (c) and 1812.608 (c), (j), (g), (i) and (j) by failing to truthfully represent the goods to be auctioned, and indeed, lying about the goods that were being auctioned, their value and/or condition as more fully set forth at length herein and above.

191.   Defendant Rosedale aided and abetted Defendant Linden in violating Cal. Civ. Code § 1812.600 et seq. by making numerous false statements in the media and to the press and, accordingly, is liable pursuant to Civ. Code § 1812.608 (b), (c), (i) and has, accordingly, committed a misdemeanor and is punishable pursuant to § 1812.604.

-38-

192.   By violating Cal. Civ. Code § 1812.600, et. seq., and pursuant to § 1812.604,

Defendant Linden is guilty of a misdemeanor.

193.   Pursuant to Cal. Civ. Code § 1812.600 (l), Plaintiff is entitled to recover a civil

penalty of $1000 for Defendants violation of the statute, an action for enforcement of those

duties, and/or recovery and such penalties should be cumulative for every infraction.

194.   Pursuant to Cal. Civ. Code § 1812.600 (m), Plaintiff is entitled to a reasonable

attorney fee and costs, in addition to the civil penalties provided for in Cal. Civ. Code §

1812.600 (l).

WHEREFORE, Plaintiff Marc Bragg prays this Honorable Court enter judgment for

Plaintiff and against Defendants Linden Research, Inc. and Philip Rosedale, for damages and

penalties pursuant to Cal. Civ. Code § 1812.600, et seq., in addition to attorneys fees and costs.

JURY TRIAL DEMANDED

COUNT VI: CONVERSION

195.   Plaintiff hereby incorporates by reference Paragraphs 1 through 194, as more fully

set forth above.

196.   Plaintiff held all title, interest and possessory rights to the virtual land, items and

intellectual property herein described that was acquired from Defendants and/or third parties

and/or created by Plaintiff and paid for using U.S. Currency.

197.   Plaintiff equally held all title, interest and possessory rights in his U.S. Currency

that was held on deposit by Defendants.

198.   The virtual property and U.S. currency described above and herein are interests

capable of precise definition, exclusive possession or control and, Plaintiff had a legitimate claim

to exclusivity of such virtual property and U.S. currency. As set forth above and herein, these

-39-

rights were secured to Plaintiff through various statements made by Defendants to and in the media, in addition to Plaintiff's exclusive possessory rights to the virtual property, items, intellectual property and U.S. Currency by and through his payment of U.S. Currency for such items.

199.   Defendants intentionally, without Plaintiff's consent and without lawful justification, interfered with and destroyed Plaintiffs right of property in, or use or possession of the goods and/or chattel as more fully set forth above and herein.

200.   The interference with and disposition of Plaintiff's rights were wrongful and caused Plaintiff damages.

201.   Defendants did not refund or otherwise return the consideration paid for the property. Moreover, Defendants, re-auctioned Plaintiff's virtual property and retained all the benefit of such auctions of their own good and unjust enrichment.

202.   Plaintiff is entitled to money damages amounting to the full value of the chattel which has been wrongfully converted by the Defendants.

WHEREFORE, Plaintiff Marc Bragg prays this Honorable Court enter judgment for Plaintiff and against Defendants Linden Research, Inc. and Philip Rosedale, for actual damages, for Defendants' conversion in an amount that the Court determines is proper and just including costs.

JURY TRIAL DEMANDED

COUNT VII: INTENTIONAL INTERFERENCE WITH A CONTRACTUAL RELATIONS / PROSPECTIVE ECONOMIC ADVANTAGE

203.   Plaintiff hereby incorporates by reference Paragraphs 1 through 202, as more fully set forth above.

DOCS_PIT 35184v.1

204.   Plaintiff possessed all intellectual property rights in the virtual items he created in Second Life and had the exclusive rights to exploit such copyrights and/or intellectual property rights.

205.   Plaintiff also possessed all rights in the virtual property he bought in Second Life from Defendants and/or third parties.

206.   Plaintiff had previously and, at the time that Defendants stole his property, entered into contracts with third parties for the sale of virtual property and/or the virtual items he had created in Second Life. Further, Plaintiff had the right and/or ability to sell the virtual items he had obtained from third parties to others.

207.   Prospective contractual relations existed between Plaintiff and third parties for the sale of his virtual property and/or items, including the intellectual property he had created and/or the transfer of such rights to a third party.

208.   Defendants had knowledge of Plaintiff's rights and/or virtual land and items he possessed and of Plaintiff's past sale of such virtual items and of such prospective sales of such items and land.

209.   Defendants intentionally, without any privilege and/or justification, interfered with Plaintiff's rights to such prospective contractual relations / economic advantage.

210.   Plaintiff has been caused damages by such acts by the Defendants.

WHEREFORE, Plaintiff Marc Bragg prays this Honorable Court enter judgment for Plaintiff and against Defendants Linden Research, Inc. and Philip Rosedale, for actual damages, for Defendants' interference in an amount that the Court determines is proper and just including costs.

JURY TRIAL DEMANDED

-41-

COUNT VIII: BREACH OF CONTRACT

211. Plaintiff hereby incorporates by reference Paragraphs 1 through 210, as more fully set forth above.

212. Each of the virtual land transactions described herein and above by and between Plaintiff and Defendants was a valid and enforceable contract.

213. Plaintiff paid valuable consideration for the virtual land bought from Defendants via auction.

214. Defendants agreed to provide all right, title and interest to the virtual land as described above and herein.

215. Contrary to such agreement, Defendants did not provide such right, title and interest to the virtual land and, as such, violated the contract between the parties.

216. The agreements were written as they were executed through Defendants auction system. Attached hereto collectively as Exhibit "3," are examples of the e-mail confirmations sent confirming such transactions that occurred through Defendants' auction system.

217. Pursuant to Pa.R.C.P. 1019(i), although the claims of Plaintiff are based upon the written agreement of the parties, the writings are not all accessible to Plaintiff as Plaintiff did not retain each of the e-mail confirming the auction results. Further, the auction contract / results, which contained the actual confirmation of the contract in writing, are no longer contained on Defendants' website and/or no longer accessible by Plaintiff.

218. Instead, Defendants intentionally took acts to deprive Plaintiff of the benefit of the contract and/or frustrated his rights to receive the benefits of the agreement actually made.

219. Plaintiff has been harmed and damaged by Defendants breach of contract.

DOCS_PIT 35184v.1

220.   Each of the pieces of virtual land purchased by Plaintiff from Defendants was unique.

221.   There is no adequate remedy at law provided with regard to the purchase of the virtual land. As such, Plaintiff is entitled to equitable relief to protect his rights pursuant to the contract.

222.   Accordingly, Defendants should be ordered to convey the virtual land back to Plaintiff and should be enjoined or otherwise prevented from precluding Plaintiff from accessing and enjoying his virtual land.

223.   Defendants should also be ordered to provide access to Plaintiff such that he can exploit, enjoy and/or otherwise use his land without interruption and interference from Defendants.

WHEREFORE, Plaintiff Marc Bragg prays this Honorable Court enter judgment for Plaintiff and against Defendants Linden Research, Inc. and Philip Rosedale, for actual damages, for Defendants' breach of contract in an amount that the Court determines is proper and just including costs and equitable relief.

JURY TRIAL DEMANDED

COUNT IX: UNJUST ENRICHMENT

224.   Plaintiff hereby incorporates by reference Paragraphs 1 through 223, as more fully set forth above.

225.   Defendants not only took Plaintiff's virtual property from him, but also resold it to the highest bidder.

226.   The re-sale of the property was not governed by any written contract.

-43-

DOCS_PIT 35184v.1

227.   Defendant's sold the virtual property at auction to the highest bidder to unjustly enrich themselves at the expense of Plaintiff.

228.   At no time did Defendants remit the money they obtained in the re-auction to Plaintiff.

229.   Accordingly, Defendants are obligated to provide restitution to Plaintiff.

WHEREFORE, Plaintiff Marc Bragg prays this Honorable Court enter judgment for Plaintiff and against Defendants Linden Research, Inc. and Philip Rosedale, for actual damages in the form of restitution, for Defendants' unjust enrichment in an amount that the Court determines is proper and just including costs.

JURY TRIAL DEMANDED

COUNT X: TORTIOUS BREACH OF THE COVENANT OF GOOD FAITH AND FAIR DEALING (CALIFORNIA LAW)

230.   Plaintiff hereby incorporates by reference Paragraphs 1 through 229, as more fully set forth above.

231.   There is, implied in every contract, a covenant of good faith and fair dealing.

232.   In the contracts whereby Defendants sold virtual land to Plaintiff, there was impliedly covenanted that Defendants would, in good faith and in the exercise of fair dealing, deal with Plaintiff fairly and honestly and do nothing to impair, interfere with, hinder or potentially injure Plaintiff's rights.

233.   Plaintiff asserts this cause of action seeking contract damages for tortious breach of the implied covenant of good faith and fair dealing. Plaintiff alleges this cause of action for breach of the implied covenant of good faith and fair dealing as to that conduct of the Defendants which is determined not to be a breach of an express contractual provision but which nonetheless

DOCS_PIT 35184v.1

is contrary to the contract's purpose and Plaintiff's legitimate expectations and thereby violates the implied covenant.

234.   As more fully set forth herein and above, Defendants breached the covenant, including but not limited to:

        a.   Any and all of the Defendants' conduct as alleged above to the extent that such conduct is determined not to be a breach of any express consensual term of any contract;

        b.   Asserting an interpretation of the virtual property contracts which is contrary to the express terms of such contracts alleged above and herein and pursuant to such interpretation, the Defendants have claimed that they are no longer required to fulfill its express promises and obligations and, indeed, have frustrated the very purpose of the contracts by involuntarily taking back such virtual property for their own unjust enrichment and defeating the very purpose of the contract selling such land in the first place;

        c.   Evading the spirit of the bargain which Plaintiff made with the Defendants when they sold the virtual land to Plaintiff;

        d.   Failing to deal with Plaintiff fairly and honestly and continually taking repeated action to impair, interfere with, hinder and injure Plaintiff's rights, such conduct being more fully set forth at length herein and above; and,

        e.   Engaging in a pattern and practice of dishonesty as more fully set forth at length herein and above.

235.   Plaintiff performed under the contract as required by paying his U.S. currency for such virtual property.

236.   As a proximate result of the Defendants' acts as alleged herein, Plaintiff has been damaged in an amount according to proof at trial.

-45-

DOCS_PIT 35184v.1

237.   Plaintiff should be awarded punitive damages for the conduct of Defendants. The Defendants have specifically misrepresented the transfer of all right, title and interest to Plaintiff and the world at large in their overall scheme to defraud consumers into becoming participants of Second Life and so that Defendants can maximize their own profits.

238.   In September, 2005, Defendant Rosedale disclosed Defendants intent by announcing the policy that all membership to Second Life would become "free." The "business" reason for making the membership "free" was set forth by Rosedale in an interview with CNET News on or about September 8, 2005, wherein he stated: "We're going to make more because some of the people who wouldn't have otherwise signed up are going to buy land . . . ."

239.   The virtual land ownership lie was and remains a cornerstone of Defendants' crooked business model.

WHEREFORE, Plaintiff Marc Bragg prays this Honorable Court enter judgment for Plaintiff and against Defendants Linden Research, Inc. and Philip Rosedale, for actual and punitive damages, for Defendants' breach in an amount that the Court determines is proper and just including costs.

JURY TRIAL DEMANDED

WHITE AND WILLIAMS, LLP

By _____
Jason A. Archinaco, Esq.

Date: _10-3-06_

VERIFICATION OF COMPLAINT

I, Marc Bragg, Esq. verify that the facts set forth in the foregoing *Plaintiff's Complaint in Civil Action* are true and correct to the best of my knowledge, information and belief. I understand that false statements herein are made subject to the penalties of 18 Pa.C.S.A. § 4904 relating to unsworn falsifications to authorities.

_____
Mark Bragg, Esq.

Dated: _10/3/C6_____

-47-

What is Second Life?   Showcase   Business Partners   Developers   Support

COMMUNITY
Forums

Volunteer
Education

CONNECTIONS
Media
Blogs
Resident Sites
Newsletter
Mailing Lists
COMMERCE
Classifieds
Land Information
  Land Auctions
  Land Store
LindeX Currency Exchange

  Sell US
     Data
   Transaction History
MY SECOND LIFE
  Account
Friends Online
Feature Voting

SUPPORT
Downloads
Police Blotter
Troubleshooting

Your Account: Marc Woebegone: Land

Land

Owned Parcels

Name	Location	Size
Maekju 001 (128,128) 2048 m2 Beatiiul penninusla rent or sale.	Maekju (160,112)	4096
Hodu 001 (128,128) 1024 m2 Mature Roadside One Sim to Ocean	Hodu (176,144)	1024
Hodu 001 (128,128) 512 m2 for development of any kind.	Hodu (80,248)	512
Cupideo Slingo. Where Luck Meets the Ocean and U Win! Danpoon	Danpoon (94,62)	528
Hodu 001 (128,128) 512 m2 for development of any kind.	Hodu (108,232)	512
Ho Su 001 (128,128) Mature 1024m2 Ocean Views and Hill Tops.	Ho Su (208,48)	1024
Maekju 001 (128,128) 1024 m2 Beatiiul penninusla rent or sale.	Maekju (208,208)	1024
Ho Su 001 (128,128) Mature 4096m2 Ocean Views and Hill Tops.	Ho Su (128,48)	4096
Maekju 001 (128,128) 4096 m2 Beautiful coast penninsusa prop.	Maekju (64,64)	4096
Atlas 001 (82,48) 1904 m2	Atlas (106,72)	1904
Juree Mature 512 m2. Very buildable	Juree (176,152)	512
Ho Su 001 (128,128) Mature 1024m2 Ocean Views and Hill Tops.	Ho Su (16,240)	1024
Hodu 001 (128,128) 512 m2	Hodu (16,136)	512
Hodu 001 (128,128) 512 m2	Hodu (16,120)	512
Hodu 001 (128,128) 1152 m2 Mature Roadside One Sim to Ocean	Hodu (174,16)	1152
Hodu 001 (128,128) 1328 m2 Mature roadside	Hodu (170,208)	1328
Chamnamoo 001 (128,128) 1,024 m2 Mature	Chamnamoo (16,208)	1024
Hodu 001 (128,128) 528 m2 for development of any kind.	Hodu (80,234)	528
Hodu 001 (128,128) 256 m2	Hodu (8,248)	256
Ho Su 001 (128,128) Mature 1024m2 Ocean Views and Hill Tops.	Ho Su (16,144)	1024
Maekju 001 (128,128) 4096 m2 Beatiiul penninusla rent or sale.	Maekju (240,16)	1024

Maekju 001 (128,128) 1024 m2 Beatiiul penninusla rent or sale.	Maekju (208,240)	1024
Hodu 001 (128,128) 512 m2	Hodu (16,40)	512
Cristat (14,94) - 800 m2	Cristat (14,114)	800
Maekju 001 (128,128) 1024 m2 Beautiful coast penninsusa prop.	Maekju (16,176)	1024
Jarang 512 m2 Mature Flat Land	Jarang (40,112)	512
Maekju 001 (128,128) 1024 m2 Beatiiul penninusla rent or sale.	Maekju (144,208)	1024
Cupideo Casino, Video n Dance Club - Areumdeuli	Areumdeuli (112,248)	496
Chamnamoo 001 (128,128) 1024 m2 Mature	Chamnamoo (240,112)	1024
Ribeata (158,228) - 896 m2	Ribeata (138,238)	112
Hodu 001 (128,128) 27152 m2 for development of any kind.	Hodu (82,216)	1584
Hodu 001 (128,128) 256 m2	Hodu (8,216)	256
Hodu 001 (128,128) 1024 m2 Top of the hill. Commanding view.	Hodu (208,48)	1024
Hodu 001 (128,128) 1152 m2 Mature Roadside One Sim to Ocean	Hodu (174,176)	1152
Maekju 001 (128,128) 1024 m2 Beautiful coast penninsusa prop.	Maekju (16,80)	1024
Hodu 001 (128,128) 512 m2	Hodu (16,56)	512
Hodu 001 (128,128) 256 m2	Hodu (24,200)	256
Chamnamoo 001 (128,128) 1024 m2 Mature	Chamnamoo (240,80)	1024
Hodu 001 (128,128) 512 m2	Hodu (16,88)	512
Bembecia Mature Flat Land 640m2 Road side	Bembecia (124,114)	640
Danpoon Mature 3536 m2 Ocean View Property	Danpoon (142,214)	2512
Hodu 001 (128,128) 256 m2	Hodu (24,248)	256
Hodu 001 (128,128) 512 m2 for development of any kind.	Hodu (76,232)	512
Cupideo Video n Rave Dance Club in Danpoon	Danpoon (178,190)	560
Chamnamoo 001 (128,128) 1024 m2 Mature	Chamnamoo (208,16)	1024
Ho Su 001 (128,128) Mature 1024m2 Ocean Views and Hill Tops.	Ho Su (16,176)	1024
Chamnamoo 001 (128,128) 1056 m2 Mature	Chamnamoo (234,214)	1056
Ho Su 001 (128,128) Mature 65536m	Ho Su (240,16)	1024
Maekju 001 (128,128) 4096 m2 Beatiiul penninusla rent or sale.	Maekju (160,16)	4096
Maekju 001 (128,128) 4096 m2 Beautiful coast penninsusa prop.	Maekju (64,128)	4096
Chamnamoo 001 (128,128) 1024 m2 Mature	Chamnamoo (240,48)	1024
Maekju 001 (128,128) 4096 m2 Beatiiul penninusla rent or sale.	Maekju (160,80)	4096
Hodu 001 (128,128) 27152 m2 for	Hodu (60,200)	896

development of any kind.

Jarang 512 m2 Mature Flat Land	Jarang (80,168)	512
Songi - Mature Perfect Ocean View Property - Neg on $z n $	Songi (14,186)	336
Maekju 001 (128,128) 32768 m2 Beatiiul penninusla rent or sale.	Maekju (176,208)	1024
Maekju 001 (128,128) 4096 m2 Beatiiul penninusla rent or sale.	Maekju (240,80)	1024
Cupideo Casino Vid n Dance Club in Saeneul	Saeneul (144,216)	512
Maekju 001 (128,128) 8192 m2 Beatiiul penninusla rent or sale.	Maekju (192,160)	8192
Chamnamoo 001 (128,128) 4512 m2 Mature	Chamnamoo (204,144)	4528
Hodu 001 (128,128) 512 m2	Hodu (16,168)	512
Ho Su 001 (128,128) Mature 1024m2 Ocean Views and Hill Tops.	Ho Su (16,208)	1024
Danpoon Mature Ocean Front Property 2,048	Danpoon (228,134)	2048
Maekju 001 (128,128) 4096 m2 Beatiiul penninusla rent or sale.	Maekju (160,48)	4096
Maekju 001 (128,128) 1024 m2 Beautiful coast penninsusa prop.	Maekju (80,240)	1024
Maekju 001 (128,128) 1024 m2 Beatiiul penninusla rent or sale.	Maekju (240,240)	1024
Hodu 001 (128,128) 512 m2 for development of any kind.	Hodu (48,248)	512
Chamnamoo Prime Mature Flat Roadside Land 1,024) 1024m2	Chamnamoo (106,118)	3696
Noonkkot First Land	Noonkkot (248,240)	512
Cupideo Art Walk in Danpoon at the Breakers 6048 m2	Danpoon (58,94)	8928
Atlas 001 (82,48) 9904 m2	Atlas (134,54)	16
Cupideo Casino. SLingo, Condos, Casino and Dance in Danpoon	Danpoon (116,128)	24704
Hodu 001 (128,128) 4096 m2 Top of the hill. Commanding view.	Hodu (224,96)	4096
Wooson 1024m2 Mature Land near water	Wooson (250,200)	192
Maekju 001 (128,128) 2048 m2 Beautiful coast penninsusa prop.	Maekju (80,192)	2048
Hodu 001 (128,128) 4096 m2 Top of the hill. Commanding view	Hodu (224,224)	4096
Cupideo Video n Dance Club in Danpoon	Danpoon (184,222)	896
Wooson 1024m2 Mature Land near water	Wooson (240,208)	832
Hodu 001 (128,128) 256 m2	Hodu (24,232)	256
Chamnamoo 001 (128,128) 59232 m2	Chamnamoo (16,240)	1024
Hodu 001 (128,128) 61008 m2	Hodu (154,186)	48
Linden Land	Agamok (194,162)	16
Maekju 001 (128,128) 4096 m2 Beatiiul penninusla rent or sale.	Maekju (240,48)	1024
Hodu 001 (128,128) 1024 m2 Mature	Hodu (176,112)	1024

Roadside One Sim to Ocean

Chamnamoo 001 (128,128) 1024 m2 Mature	Chamnamoo (240,16)	1024
Maekju 001 (128,128) 4096 m2 Beatiiul penninusla rent or sale.	Maekju (112,192)	4096
Danpoon Mature 1024 m2 Ocean View Property	Danpoon (142,246)	1024
Hodu 001 (128,128) 256 m2	Hodu (8,200)	256
Hodu 001 (128,128) 448 m2 for development of any kind.	Hodu (110,248)	448
Hodu 001 (128,128) 1024 m2 Top of the hill. Commanding view.	Hodu (208,16)	1024
Hodu 001 (128,128) 512 m2	Hodu (16,104)	512
Cupideo Casino at The Breakers in Danpoon	Danpoon (228,182)	3776
Hodu 001 (128,128) 1024 m2 Top of the hill. Commanding view.	Hodu (240,48)	1024
Cupideo Casino, Vid n Dance Club - Dotoorak	Dotoorak (216,48)	432
Cristat (148,124) - 544 m2	Cristat (160,136)	160
Maekju 001 (128,128) 1024 m2 Beautiful coast penninsusa prop.	Maekju (48,176)	1024
Hodu 001 (128,128) 512 m2	Hodu (16,152)	512
Hodu 001 (128,128) 512 m2	Hodu (16,72)	512
Chamnamoo 001 (128,128) 3136 Roadside Mature	Chamnamoo (128,102)	3136
Maekju 001 (128,128) 2048 m2 Beatiiul penninusla rent or sale.	Maekju (240,112)	1024
Maekju 001 (128,128) 2048 m2 Beautiful coast penninsusa prop.	Maekju (16,32)	2048
Hodu 001 (128,128) 1024 m2 Top of the hill. Commanding view.	Hodu (240,16)	1024
Hodu 001 (128,128) 1504 m2 mature roadside near ocean sim	Hodu (168,240)	1504
Maekju 001 (128,128) 2048 m2 Beautiful coast penninsusa prop.	Maekju (16,128)	2048

https://secondlife.com/account/land.php   5/9/2006

WHAT IS SECOND LIFE?   SHOWCASE   BUSINESS PARTNERS   DEVELOPERS   COMMUNITY   SUPPORT

COMMUNITY
Forums
Events
Volunteer
Education
CONNECTIONS
Media
Blogs
Resident Sites
Newsletter
Mailing Lists
COMMERCE
Classifieds
Land Information
  • Land Auctions
  • Land Store
Lindex Currency Exchange
  • Buy L$
  • Sell L$
  • Lindex Market Data
  • Transaction History
Economic Statistics [NEW!]
MY SECOND LIFE
My Account
Friends Online
Feature Voting
Refer-A-Friend
Partners
SUPPORT
Downloads
Police Blotter
Troubleshooting

Your Account: Marc Woebegone: Land

Land

You do not own any parcels.

downloads | system requirements | privacy | community standards | terms of service | dmca | grid status | jobs

https://secondlife.com/account/land.php   5/15/2006

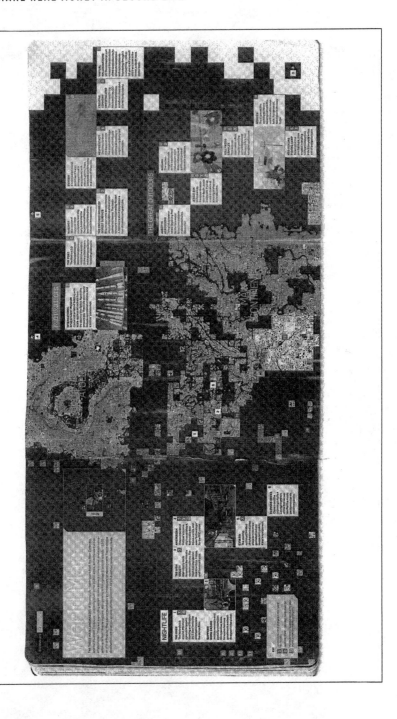

Main Identity

From: <land@secondlife.com>
To: <msb@lawy-ers.com>
Sent: Saturday, February 25, 2006 4:00 PM
Subject: Second Life Auction: Item Won! Cristat (14,94) - 1792 m2

Congratulations Marc Woebegone!

You have agreed to purchase the following item from Second Life:

Auction ID: 0026198057
Item: Cristat (14,94) - 1792 m2
Winning Bid: L$9,010

Please go to the below link and pay for your auction:
http://secondlife.com/auctions/detail.php?id=0026198057

You will need to go in-world and claim the land within seven days. If you encounter a problem, email land@secondlife.com.

Please note: be sure to have enough land tier available before claiming your land, or you will be prompted to tier-up.

Linden Lab and the Second Life Team
http://www.secondlife.com

EXHIBIT

3

6/9/2006

Main Identity

From:	\<land@secondlife.com\>
To:	\<msb@lawy-ers.com\>
Sent:	Monday, February 27, 2006 3:55 PM
Subject:	Second Life Auction: Billing Failure

Congratulations Marc Woebegone!

You have agreed to purchase the following item from Second Life:

Auction ID: 0026198076
Item: Songi - 001 - 65536 m2
Winning Bid: US$1605.00

Unfortunately we were unable to bill your account. In order to correct
this problem, please review your Membership and billing information to
ensure that everything is accurate and up to date. If the information you
have listed is accurate and correct, you may wish to contact your bank or
credit card issuer or paypal (depending on your payment method). Common
errors include mismatched addresses, expired credit cards and incorrect
expiration dates. Please contact land@secondlife.com within seven days if
you do not wish to forfeit this item.

To review or modify your account details, or to change or cancel your
Membership Plan, visit https://secondlife.com/account.

Linden Lab and the Second Life Team
http://www.secondlife.com

6/9/2006

Main Identity

From:	<land@secondlife.com>
To:	<msb@lawy-ers.com>
Sent:	Tuesday, February 28, 2006 11:02 PM
Subject:	Second Life Auction: Item Won! Ribeata (158,228) - 5104 m2

Congratulations Marc Woebegone!

You have agreed to purchase the following item from Second Life:

Auction ID: 0026198022
Item: Ribeata (158,228) - 5104 m2
Winning Bid: L$32,010

Please go to the below link and pay for your auction:
http://secondlife.com/auctions/detail.php?id=0026198022

You will need to go in-world and claim the land within seven days. If you encounter a problem, email land@secondlife.com.

Please note: be sure to have enough land tier available before claiming your land, or you will be prompted to tier-up.

Linden Lab and the Second Life Team
http://www.secondlife.com

6/9/2006

Main Identity

From:	<land@secondlife.com>
To:	<msb@lawy-ers.com>
Sent:	Thursday, April 13, 2006 7:11 AM
Subject:	Second Life Auction: Item Won! Ho Su 001 (128,128) Mature 65536m

Congratulations Marc Woebegone!

You have agreed to purchase the following item from Second Life:

Auction ID: 0026198344
Item: Ho Su 001 (128,128) Mature 65536m
Winning Bid: US$1,501

Please go to the below link and pay for your auction:

http://secondlife.com/auctions/detail.php?id=0026198344

You will need to go in-world and claim the land within two days. If you
encounter a problem, email land@secondlife.com.

Please note: be sure to have enough land tier available before claiming
your land, or you will be prompted to tier-up.

Linden Lab and the Second Life Team
http://www.secondlife.com

6/9/2006

SELECTED
SECOND LIFE
EARLY
ADOPTERS

No list of the companies, agencies, and organizations occupying space on the platform can be complete, and the one that follows is far from being so. But it should give you a picture of the range of entities that have made a calculation that Second Life is a space they need to be in, for one reason or another. Among the companies I've left off the list are those whose brand has a presence in the environment but which don't maintain a permanent corporate presence, at least they didn't as of early 2007. Coca-Cola comes to mind. When you're on the platform, you see Coca-Cola vending machines all over the place, but when you search for the company in the in-world search engine, nothing comes up. Adidas is another one.

I've listed each company with its SLURL (Second Life URL), so you can get to each site from your Web browser as long as you have Second Life downloaded and running on your computer.

Consumer and Durable Goods

American Apparel (offline since mid-2007)
http://slurl.com/secondlife/Lerappa/133/102/24/

Bantam Books
http://slurl.com/secondlife/SheepIsland/122/31/25

BMW
http://slurl.com/secondlife/BMWNewWorld/196/66/23

Calvin Klein
http://slurl.com/secondlife/Avalon/21/146/45

Circuit City
http://slurl.com/secondlife/IBM10/142/35/23

Mercedes
http://slurl.com/secondlife/MercedesBenzIsland/128/128/0

Nintendo
http://slurl.com/secondlife/SeventhEye/152/113/35

Nissan
http://slurl.com/secondlife/NissanAltima/122/181/28

Pontiac
http://slurl.com/secondlife/Pontiac/142/91/24

Reebok
http://slurl.com/secondlife/Reebok/133/148/100

Starwood
http://slurl.com/secondlife/Argali/128/128/0

Toyota
http://slurl.com/secondlife/ScionCity/48/39/23

Technology

Advanced Micro Devices (AMD)
http://slurl.com/secondlife/AMDDevCentral/104/176/25

Dell
http://slurl.com/secondlife/DellIsland4/3/162/24

IBM
http://slurl.com/secondlife/IBM/106/6/23

Intel
http://slurl.com/secondlife/Thomson/20/90/0

Sony
http://slurl.com/secondlife/Media/166/80/46

Sun Microsystems
http://slurl.com/secondlife/SunPavilion/167/157/91

Telus
http://slurl.com/secondlife/Shinda/187/72/22

Thomson NETg (Training)
http://slurl.com/secondlife/Thomson/184/119/35

Services

Coldwell Banker
http://slurl.com/secondlife/Ranchero/210/229/32

H&R Block
http://slurl.com/secondlife/HRBlock/112/50/38

Leo Burnett (advertising)
http://slurl.com/secondlife/Leo Burnett/162/93/34

PA Consulting (U.K. management consultant)
http://slurl.com/secondlife/PAconsulting/116/119/27

Media

CNET Networks
http://slurl.com/secondlife/MillionsofUs/227/30/38

Reuters
http://slurl.com/secondlife/Reuters/126/100/25

Weather Channel
http://slurl.com/secondlife/Weather/113/5/26

Wired
http://slurl.com/secondlife/MillionsofUs/203/228/23

Agencies and Organizations

American Library Association
http://slurl.com/secondlife/ALAArtsInfoIsland/146/123/56

Global Kids (urban youth charity)
http://slurl.com/secondlife/Cincta/80/105/32

National Oceanic and Atmospheric Administration (NOAA)
http://slurl.com/secondlife/Meteora/177/161/27

New York University
http://slurl.com/secondlife/Campus/68/120/0

San Jose State School of Library and Information Sciences
http://slurl.com/secondlife/SJSUSLIS/128/128/0

SELECTED SECOND LIFE **DEVELOPMENT** AND **MARKETING** CONSULTANTS

There are dozens of firms and dozens of individuals who can be tapped to help you launch and target your Second Life presence, certainly more than I could hope to provide here. To give you a starting place for finding professional assistance, I've listed about a dozen consultants. The fact that I've listed some here isn't an endorsement of their services and shouldn't be taken as a suggestion that they do the best work. I've listed them only because I know

about them by talking to them, through material I've read about them, or by simply stumbling upon something they've built. There are many good design and marketing consultants not included, so it would make sense to ask about others as you familiarize yourself with the platform.

The first three I've listed are widely regarded as the big players in the field, I think that's fair to say. As you'll see, each has worked on major builds, and you can judge for yourself whether examples of their work demonstrate a design quality or functionality that is close to what you have in mind for your own project. Beyond them, I've included a few other consultants whose work you can check out. Some are more developers than marketers, and some are more marketers than developers, but it's a safe bet that any of them can help you to find assistance if their particular specialty leaves gaps in the kind of help you need.

As for pricing, no consultant I interviewed felt comfortable giving fees because of all the pricing variables, but they all said that development costs are comparable to costs for professional Web development services. One executive of a major 3-D development firm was quoted in press coverage as saying that an initial build, for a major custom project, costs from $75,000 to $100,000. But as we've seen, it's also possible to get in for very little if your project can be developed appropriately for your needs using off-the-shelf objects and applications.

The Big Three

The Electric Sheep Company (Washington, D.C.)
www.electricsheepcompany.com
Selected Second Life clients: Major League Baseball, Reuters, Starwood aloft

Millions of Us (Sausalito, California)
www.millionsofus.com
Selected Second Life clients: CNET Networks, Intel, Sun Microsystems, Toyota, *Wired*

Rivers Run Red (San Francisco)
www.riversrunred.com
Selected Second Life clients: Adidas, BBC, Calvin Klein, Heineken, ING, Penguin, Reebok, Vodaphone

Selected Others (Development, Consulting, or Marketing)

The Ad Option (TAO)
www.ad-option.com
Selected clients, builds, or projects: American Apparel, New York

Aimee Weber
www.aimeeweber.com
Selected clients, builds, or projects: American Apparel, Midnight City, NOAA, New Globe Theater, Save the Children

Apple MacKay
www.applemackay.com
Selected clients, builds, or projects: Wiichi Studio

Bizarre Fish Studio
www.bizzarefishstudio.com
Selected clients, builds, or projects: Technocity, Penny Lane Mall

Catalyst
www.ctly.net
Selected clients, builds, or projects: AdBoards

Clear Ink
www.clearink.com
Selected clients, builds, or projects: Autodesk Island, model U.S. Capitol

Cranial Tap
www.cranialtap.com
Selected clients, builds, or projects: Costa del Sol Resort, Lake Citrago

Crayon
www.crayonville.com
Selected clients, builds, or projects: Coca-Cola

ibranz
www.ibranz.com
Selected clients, builds, or projects: ibranz headquarters, Cheyenne Mountain Bookstores, Cheerful Givers

MojoZoo
www.mojozoo.com
Selected clients, builds, or projects: Books for Soldiers

Reperes Second Life (research, Paris-based)
www.reperes-secondlife.com
Selected clients, builds, or projects: Research surveys: resident purchase habits, perceptions

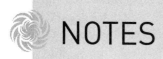

NOTES

Supporting material and references are organized under the same headings that appear in the text.

CHAPTER 1: IF YOU HAVEN'T HEARD ABOUT SECOND LIFE, YOU WILL, SO WHAT'S IT ALL ABOUT?

It took a few years after its launch for the platform to really catch on. As recently as early 2005, roughly two years after it launched, the platform had just 100,000 residents [http://lindenlab.com/press/releases/01_06_06], while World of Warcraft had a subscriber base nearing 7 million: http://www.joystiq.com/2006/09/07/world-of-warcraft-hits-7-million-subscribers/. As of mid-2007, World of Warcraft continued to have more subscribers, but Second Life's rate of growth by then had what can only be described as an explosion, growing to almost 5.5 million in about two and a half years. That growth rate has been driven by a few developments, but it certainly has at its foundation the one key step Linden Lab took in late 2003, at a time when the mainstream media weren't following what it was doing closely: giving residents intellectual property rights to the objects they create [http://lindenlab.com/press/releases/03_11_14]. Then, in mid-2006 Linden Lab took the step of allowing subscribers to open "unverified" accounts, that is, accounts in which subscribers didn't need to disclose their credit card number: http://www.secondlifeherald.com/slh/2006/12/ avatar_of_the_y_1.html. And then in early 2007 it released its source code to anyone who wanted it, making it a completely open platform, something of interest to developers: http://lindenlab.com/press/releases/01_08_07. Storm Williams of MojoZoo calls the unverified accounts one of the triggering events for the platform's stunning growth.

The platform has received a lot of positive coverage in the business press. Here's an article that's representative, from *Fortune*: http://money.cnn.com/2006/11/09/technology/fastforward_secondlife.fortune/index.htm?postversion=2006111011. It's this piece in which *Fortune's* "not overhyped" comment appears.

Here's a *BusinessWeek* article: http://www.businessweek.com/ magazine/content/06_47/b4010068.htm. And here's a *USA Today* article, http://www.usatoday.com/money/advertising/2006-12-06-marketers-second-life_x.htm.

I say that Second Life started out primarily as a playground for computer geeks based on where most of the platform's early coverage came from: computer publications like Gamespot.com, Gamespy.com, *Red Herring*, FutureLooks.com, *PC Magazine*, *Wired News*, and *Game Set Watch*. You can read some of these early articles at the news coverage archive at the Linden Lab site: http://secondlife.com/news/.

Time to Hang Your Shingle

When I talk about asphalt parking lots, I'm referring to real asphalt parking lots, at least in a visual sense. One of the ways Second Life gets its interesting visual effects is through the use of imported photo files. Actual photographs of asphalt parking lots are imported into the system by developers and are used to decorate raw "prims," the building blocks of Second Life objects. Although everything has a cartoon look to it, the cartoons are based on photographs of real textures

You can see some of the platform's growth trajectory on the Second Life Web site, where the growth of its premium account holders is charted: http://secondlife.com/whatis/economy-graphs.php.

What Kind of Shingle Should You Hang?

The statistics are ever-changing, but if you want to get a snapshot of the platform's "gross domestic product," you can check out the charts at Second Life's Web site: http://secondlife.com/whatis/ economy_stats.php.

The $1.5 million in daily transaction volume was an often-quoted number in mid-2007. Here's an example: http://blog.cleveland.com/ earlyedition/2007/03/artslife_want_a_second_life_it.html.

The Saint Lucia 2006 GDP is from the World Bank, the findings of which Wikepedia summarized: http://en.wikipedia.org/wiki/List_of_ countries_by_GDP_(PPP)/.

Right now, buzz is the main, if not the only, in-world currency most real-world companies in Second Life are earning. There's no better example than the pile of free media coverage American Apparel received for its in-world debut. Just search "American Apparel AND Second Life" in Google and you'll get a sense of the volume of coverage the company received.

The Web site for San Ruffino Townhomes, which Clayton was marketing in Second Life, is at http://www.sanruffinotownhomes.com/.

So much has been written on the concept of the social Internet that I'm not sure what the best reference article is, so I can probably do no better than to suggest as a starting point *Time* magazine's story on its 2006 Person of the Year, which is you (and me), since we're all content creators now: http://www.time.com/time/magazine/article/0,9171,1569514,00.html.

CHAPTER 2: THE BASICS, OR WHY PEOPLE TAKE THEIR SECOND CHANCE ON SECOND LIFE SO SERIOUSLY

You can find a directory of "massively multiplayer role-playing games" at http://www.mpogd.com/games/massively.asp?first=A. Access the SLURL site at www.slurl.com.

How You Get to This Point

The issue Arlene Ciroula raises about credit card numbers and credibility is an important one. One of the concerns people had when Linden Lab in 2006 allowed "unverified" accounts—that is, accounts in which residents didn't have to give Linden Lab their credit card number—was that residents who violated platform rules and protocols and were banned could return to the platform under a new account, creating a population of serial violators. In one blog entry, note the use of the phrase "throwaway accounts for griefing:" http://www.secondlifeherald.com/slh/2006/12/avatar_of_the_y_1.html.

You can get an up-to-date look at the conversion rate of a Linden dollar to the U.S. dollar at http://secondlife.com/whatis/economy-market.php.

I don't know if Dave Levinson of Cranial Tap is the first person to describe the Second Life economy as thriving but depressed, but he's the person from whom I heard the term "depressed," which seems a perfectly apt description of the economic life of the platform. There's a Wikipedia entry that discusses the link between depressed economies and hyperinflation, which is really what a 270:1 exchange rate is. The Wikipedia entry is at http://en.wikipedia.org/wiki/Hyperinflation.

Probably the biggest spender in Second Life so far is IBM. I can't say exactly how much it has spent, but it has publicly announced plans to apply some $10 million to a division devoted to virtual platforms, and Second Life was certainly its big early test case: http://secondlife.reuters.com/stories/2006/11/09/ibm-accelerates-push-into-3d-virtual-worlds/.

Here's what Linden Lab says you need in your computer to make Second Life work for you:

1. Internet connection: cable or DSL.
2. Operating system: Windows XP (Service Pack 2), or Windows 2000 (Service Pack 4). Note: Second Life doesn't currently support Windows Vista.
3. Computer processor: 800MHz Pentium III or Athlon or better.
4. Computer memory: 256MB or better.
5. Video/graphics card: nVidia GeForce 2, GeForce 4mx, or better, or ATI Radeon 8500, 9250, or better. (Source: http://secondlife.com/corporate/sysreqs.php.)

Before I could get onto the platform in the right way, I needed to replace my graphics card. The one I chose was the ATI Radeon 9250, which I bought in late 2006 for about $70 at CompUSA. I don't have anything with which to compare it, but it seems to work well. To install it, I spent about $200 with Geeks on Call, a national chain of IT helpers, although the installation isn't hard to do on your own if you're comfortable with computers.

Second Life's search engine is robust in the sense that pretty much everything in the world is listed in it, but it doesn't search well if you don't know the exact name of the location you want. If you search under "places" and type in only a portion of the name of an area, for example, the chances of the place coming up in the search result isn't good.

What Do You Need to Know, and Why Do You Need to Know It?

It's possible DietAdvisor Vella won't be in business by the time this book comes out. She had just launched her business when I talked with her in March 2007, and she hadn't started to make money yet. She said that she wasn't planning to proceed indefinitely with her diet advice business if she didn't start attracting customers within a few months.

Separating Yourself from Your Avatar

You can get all the information on Anshe Chung you want at her Web site, which links to much of the news coverage about her business: http://www.anshechung.com/index.php?fct=MEDIA.

You can read the *Washington Post's* coverage of Veronica Brown online: http://www.washingtonpost.com/wp-dyn/content/article/2006/12/25/AR2006122500635.html.

Again, get all the latest on the platform's gross domestic product at http://secondlife.com/whatis/economy_stats.php.

American Samoa 2006 GDP is from the CIA World Factbook, which was summarized on Wikipedia: http://en.wikipedia.org/wiki/List_of_countries_by_GDP_(PPP).

In terms of the platform's demographic profile, it's not a simple matter to piece together, and confidentiality issues play into this. But results of self-selected surveys are available. In any case, the growth of international residents is pretty widely discussed in articles and blog entries on Second Life, and a good place to start for demographic information, as of January 2007, is the official Linden blog: http://blog.secondlife.com/2007/02/09/state-of-the-virtual-world-%E2%80%93-key-metrics-january-2007/.

Statistics showing consumers tuning out TV and other media are plentiful. Here's a piece that shows some of what's going on: http://www.commercialalert.org/news/featured-in/2003/10/media-marketing-advertising-aol-aims-to-break-out-of-the-box-fresh-ad-funds-target-ways-to-reach-tv-viewers-tuning-out-commercials.

CHAPTER 3: AVOIDING THE THIRD RAIL OF SECOND LIFE: FIRST STEPS

Don't Expect Too Much

1. MATCH YOUR AMBITION TO THE SYSTEM'S CAPACITY

Here are a few pieces on Second Life's grid capacity problems and also some stats on how many servers it's using: (1) http://news.com.com/Second+Life+Dont+worry,+we+can+scale/2100-1043_3-6080186.html, (2) http://www.computerworld.com/blogs/node/5122, (3) http://linux.about.com/b/a/257654.htm.

An article from February 2007 in *The Register*, a U.K. publication, is critical of Second Life's grid capacity and indeed thinks this and some other shortcomings will doom it from becoming a place for companies to set up shop profitably: http://www.theregister.co.uk/2007/02/20second_life_analysis/.

2. REMEMBER THAT MOST AVATARS TODAY ARE STILL JUST PLAYING A GAME

Gorean fantasy life isn't for everyone. If you want to learn more, you might start with these encyclopedia entries on it: http://www.gor.net/encyclopedia.html.

3. You Can't Escape Taxes, Even in Second Life
There are several articles on the taxation issues that Congress is looking into, at least at the staff level. Here's one: http://money.cnn.com/2007/03/02/technology/sl_taxes/index.htm.

Learn more about the tier system here: http://secondlife.com/whatis/landpricing.php.

Don't Take Away the Fun

4. People Are Looking for Things to Do
A look at Linden Lab's curb on in-world gambling operations, and the extent such operations fueled the platform's economy up to that point, is included in an August 16, 2007, CFO.com report. You can read the report at http://www.cfo.com/article.cfm/9670900/c_9644880?f=singlepage.

Hewlett-Packard as the biggest computer maker is detailed in this CNET coverage: http://news.com.com/Global+PC+shipments+grow,+but+revenue+remains+flat/2100-1003_3-6150991.html.

7. "Griefing" Happens, Too; It's Another Thing You Can't Avoid
You can read about the griefing attack on Anshe Chung's press conference at http://secondlife.reuters.com/stories/2007/01/15/youtube-shift-on-anshe-chung-griefing-video/.

8. This Could All End Tomorrow
Here's information on investment into Linden Lab by Amazon's Jeff Bezos and Lotus's Mitch Kapor: http://www.siliconbeat.com/entries/2006/03/28/linden_lab_raises_11_million_to_go_more_mainstream.html.

CHAPTER 4: A FEW WORDS ABOUT MARKETS, THE LAW, LABOR, AND BANKS

Second Life's Three Markets: Currency, Real Estate, and Equities

Currency
Linden Lab says the following about its money: "Second Life 'currency' is a limited license right available for purchase or free distribution at Linden Lab's discretion, and is not redeemable for monetary value from Linden Lab." After a bit more on this point, it talks about trading your

currency: "Second Life offers an exchange, called LindeX, for the trading of Linden Dollars, which uses the terms 'buy' and 'sell' to indicate the transfer of license rights to use Linden Dollars." (Source: http://second life.com/corporate/tos.php.)

Saxo Bank's trading plans are detailed in coverage by Reuters: http://secondlife.reuters.com/stories/2007/03/02/danish-bank-moves-to-offer-trading-in-second-life/.

REAL ESTATE

Second Life keeps track of islands added per month, and it maintains a running total of the number of islands owned by the residents: http://second life.com/whatis/economy_stats.php.

Cost of a new island in mid-2007: $1,675, plus $295 in monthly land fees for maintenance. An island is 65,536 square meters, or about 16 acres: http://secondlife.com/community/land-islands.php.

The sale of the Amsterdam sims received a lot of coverage, in part because one of the popular features of the region is its robust adult businesses. Here's an example of the coverage of the sale: http://www.informationweek.com/management/showArticle.jhtml?articleID=198700237.

The identity of a Dutch media company as the buyer was noted, among other places, in a July 4, 2007, report on Mashable, a social networking news site: http://mashable.com/2007/07/04/second-life-sexbed/.

EQUITIES

The merger between the World Stock Exchange and the Metaverse Stock Exchange is covered by Reuters: http://secondlife.reuters.com/stories/2007/02/13/rival-second-life-stock-exchanges-merge/.

LukeConnell Vandevere's quote about the transparency issue is from Reuters: http://secondlife.reuters.com/stories/2007/01/ 12/hope-capital-launches-rival-to-metaverse-stock-exchange/.

The report of theft at the World Stock Exchange was reported in an August 16, 2007, piece on CFO.com, the online sister to *CFO Magazine*, called "When virtual crises turn real." I haven't independently validated the report, which appears at http://www.cfo.com/article.cfm/9670900/c_9644880?f=singlepage.

A Note on the Legal Status of Anything You Create in Second Life

There are many articles in which lawyers muse about what ownership means in Second Life. Here's a good article on the subject: http://www.

law.com/jsp/article.jsp?id=1170237755271. http://news.com.com/Second
+Life+faces+threat+to+its+virtual+economy/2100-1043_3-6135699.html.

A report on the "Sexbed Stealer" was posted on Mashable, a social networking news site, in July 2007: http://mashable.com/2007/07/04/second-life-
sexbed/.

A typical article on the copybot controversy is this one by CNET:
http://news.com.com/Second+Life+faces+threat+to+its+virtual+
economy/2100-1043_3-6135699.html.

Yes, There Are Banks

Ginko Financial's Web site lists its deposit balance: https://ginkofinancial.
com/.

Ginko's financial troubles were reported, among other places, on
CFO.com, the online sister to *CFO Magazine*, in a piece called "When virtual crises turn real," which appears at http://www.cfo.com/article.
cfm/9670900/c_9644880?f=singlepage.

CHAPTER 5: A LOOK AT SOME TEST MODELS

The Anti-Cool Approach, or
How an Accounting Firm Becomes Hip

There's another accounting firm in Second Life, Choquette & Co. Accounting Group in British Columbia, but despite repeated attempts, I wasn't able
to access its in-world location, so I'm guessing it's under development.

Jnana, the company providing the decision-tree software, maintains
a Web site at www.jnana.com.

Taming the Wild West in Real Estate

Young's first quote, on whether using virtual tours in Second Life for future real-world home sales is viable, is from a press release issued August
2, 2007. The rest of his quotes are from a conversation I had with him a
few months earlier.

Directions on accessing Second Life and getting to the Mercer Island
house are on the Web page of the Coldwell Banker agent listing the
house, Suzanne Lane. The URL is http://www.coldwellbanker.com/servlet/
PropertyListing?action=detail&ComColdwellbankerDataProperty_id=114
40843&page=property/.

They "Saw It in Second Life": The Real Estate Bridge from In-World to Your World

If you're a fan, here's a place to read about Ben Folds's performance at Starwood's virtual aloft hotel: http://www.virtualaloft.com/.

Here's *BusinessWeek* coverage of what Starwood was striving to accomplish with its virtual walk-through: http://www.virtualaloft.com/2006/08/businessweek_on_virtual_aloft.php.

Social Internet 3.0 in 3-D Space

This site has details on how the RatePoint Second Life system is intended to work: http://secondlife.ratepoint.com/sl.

Giving Universal Design a Whole New Meaning

A good place to learn about universal design is the Center for Universal Design at North Carolina State University: http://www.design.ncsu.edu/cud/.

With Promo Blast, Marketing Floodgates Open

It's pretty clear that American Apparel was the first retailer, and maybe even the first company, to set up in Second Life, but a handful of other real-life businesses can boast of at least having a temporary presence there before the clothing store. Warner Bros. and Twentieth Century Fox both held events on the platform before American Apparel's arrival:
http://www.forbes.com/technology/2006/06/14/american-apparel-retail_cz_ph_0614secondlife.html.

Among the coverage of the protest staged at American Apparel's launch party is this piece from the *Second Life Herald*: http://www.secondlifeherald.com/slh/2006/08/aftermath_of_sl.html.

It's true that Second Life's visuals aren't as stunning as those in other virtual games like World of Warcraft, but as so many analysts point out, that's the trade-off you get when you create a platform on which anyone can build. As Dave Levinson of Cranial Tap mentioned to me, you have teams of professionals designing everything you see in World of Warcraft, while in Second Life you have professional and amateur designers trying to develop things that the platform might or might not be able to accommodate efficiently, so the system is strained in all sort of ways: "Everything is user-generated content," he says, "so its susceptible to people writing scripts that can actually break the system. These users are fully exploiting the platform in ways the company could never even dream of."

CHAPTER 6: THE STARTING POINT FOR YOU

5. Market Your Space in a Way That Makes Sense

Here's a sample of some Second Life publications (or publications devoted to it). Note that these are not in-world publications; if you want to identify some of them, you can find them in the search engine on the platform.

Second Life Herald: http://www.secondlifeherald.com/

New World Notes: www.nwn.blogs.com

Second Life News: Network slnn.com

Reuters Second Life: www.secondlife.reuters.com

APPENDIX B: SELECTED SECOND LIFE DEVELOPMENT AND MARKETING CONSULTANTS

The $75,000 to $100,000 for major 3-D development work was quoted in a February 26, 2007, AP story: http://www.organic.com/about/news_detail.jsp?815.

INDEX

ACKNOWLEDGMENTS

I've never been an enthusiastic user of technology, so I would seem to be the last person in the world to write about Second Life, a virtual platform that up until two years ago was almost exclusively the domain of bona fide techies, or at least hard-core gamers. But like Nixon going to China, it's necessary for someone like me to understand and master the platform if it's going to fulfill its promise as the new face of the Internet. Looked at in this way, there probably isn't a better type of writer than the one I represent to undertake a short book on whether you should try to get your business into this environment. The fact is, if I can become comfortable with navigating the environment and mastering it enough to understand some of its nuances, then anyone can. And that's the first step toward winning the embrace of a platform by the masses: Can anyone use it? I would say the answer is yes. Your first step, then, is to learn about it yourself, and I hope this modest attempt to explain it is helpful to you in that regard.

I want to thank the people who shared their insight with me. Of course, any factual errors or faulty analysis is my responsibility alone, but without their willingness to examine the platform with me, I wouldn't have had much to say: Chris Bailey, Arlene Ciroula, John Clayton, "Naughty Desoto," Mark Friedman, Stevan Lieberman, Dave Levinson, David Marine, Bill Nissim, John Paul, Raz Schionning, Phillip Torrone, "DietAdvisor Vella," Storm Williams, and Charlie Young.

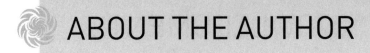

ABOUT THE AUTHOR

Robert Freedman is a 20-year veteran business reporter with a concentration in residential and commercial real estate (and with this book, virtual real estate). He is a past president of the American Society of Business Publication Editors, and is editor of three books: *Journalism that Matters* (with Steven Roll; Marion Street Press, 2006), a collection of industry-changing examples of trade journalism; *Broker to Broker* (John Wiley & Sons, 2006), a compilation of residential real estate brokerage best practices; and *Best Practices of the Business Press* (Kendall-Hunt, 2004), a look at outstanding trade publication editing. Robert is based in the Washington, D.C., area and is senior editor at *Realtor* magazine, published by the National Association of Realtors.